RECENT TRENDS IN LIBRARIES IN NETWORKED ENVIRONMENT

Challenges and Opportunities for Librarianship in 21st Century

RECENT TRENDS IN LIBRARIES IN NETWORKED ENVIRONMENT

Challenges and Opportunities for Librarianship in 21st Century

Editor in Chief
ADITYA TRIPATHI

Editors
MOHD SHOAIB ANSARI
JITENDRA KUMAR GUPTA

Ess Ess Publications
New Delhi

RECENT TRENDS IN LIBRARIES IN NETWORKED ENVIRONMENT
Challenges and Opportunities for Librarianship in 21st Century

ISBN: 978-93-87698-02-4

First Published 2018

Published by:
Ess Ess Publications
4831/24, Ansari Road,
Darya Ganj,
New Delhi-110 002.
INDIA
Phones: 23260807, 41563444
Fax: 41563334
E-mail: info@essessreference.com
www.essessreference.com

Cover Design by *Patch Creative Unit*

Printed and bound in India

Contents

Preface

The fifth law of Library Science enunciates *Library is a growing organism,* which implies that library must grow over a period of time in terms of space, users and resources. The said changes need to be addressed by adopting new methods and advancements in technologies used. The utilization of Information Communication Technologies (ICTs) in libraries has reformed the customary idea of libraries from a 'store house of books' to a 'scholarly information centre'. It has changed the entire idea of library and information centre and encouraged individuals to worldwide access of information on pocket mobile devices.

ICT has affected each and every facet of libraries particularly collection development, improved Information Retrieval System, library building and architecture and resource sharing. ICT has dramatically oriented the users to *WWW* and compelled libraries to look for new applications for access management, library collaborations and resource sharing. Availability of digital contents impelled libraries to think for rights management and user's management. New manpower must be created through capacity building programs keep the work-force as well as the clients abreast with emerging networked environment and the changing technologies.

This book means to acquaint the reader with basic

concerns and prominent issues in the field of library and information science in the networked environment. This book presents views and experiences of professionals for the larger benefit of the readers. This book is an annotation of important contemporary themes in the field of LIS. The articles in the book from different themes that would enrich the knowledge of readers in library and information science and in allied disciplines.

The content of this book is broadly divided into 11 units containing 21 articles. These are: Internet and Role of World Wide Web, Mobile Technologies, Library Resources and Services, Social Media Analysis, Digital Libraries and Institutional Repositories, Green Library and Green Computing, Library Automation and Library Consortia, Security Systems in the Libraries, MOOCs and Libraries, Changing Pattern of Library Profession, TQM in Libraries and Bibliometric Studies.

Finally, the book covers a wide assortment of issues identified with its theme, both theoretical and practical dimensions. Most of the chapters are research papers and contain very significant findings. We hope that this intellectual work would be a valuable wellspring of reference for researchers, library professionals and individuals.

We express our gratitude to the author for their helpful commitments for this book. We are also grateful to all individuals from publication and reviewer team for all the efforts and pain they have taken during the editing and reviewing process.

- Editors

1

Internet : A Boon to Fulfill Information Need

Amandeep Kaur
Assistant Librarian
DAV University, Jalandhar-Pathankot National Highway (NH 44) Jalandhar-144001 Punjab

ABSTRACT

Internet is playing very effective role in ICT era. It is a tool which is very important for accessing information at the global level. Internet is an efficient technology, which is useful for communication, dissemination and information retrieval. Internet connects the persons on a single platform which share their ideas and thoughts. In the libraries; internet plays a very important role to retrieve useful information for their users. A large number of resources are consulted by the libraries through the Internet. It is very essential in the libraries to stay connected with the whole world. The present paper presents the all the aspects of the Internet and the study is very helpful for the libraries.

Keywords : Internet, WWW, ICT, Networks, Google, E-Books, e-Journals.

INTRODUCTION

In the present era, computer is being used in every sphere of life like communication, searching information, handling data, collection, preservation, and calculation of desire figure etc. The Internet is a global network connecting millions of computers. More than 190 countries are linked into exchanges of data, news and opinions. According to Internet Live Stats, there was an estimated 3,037,608,300 Internet users worldwide as of December 30, 2014. The number of Internet users represents nearly 40 percent of the world's population. The largest number of Internet users by country is China, followed by the United States and India. The World Wide Web currently represents the single most important common interface from which one can access adverse and desperate range of information on various topics. It can become the best source of information for any field of study. We can search various sites on various subjects to gather information about a topic without any hindrance.

ARE WEB AND INTERNET THE SAME?

The Internet is not synonymous with World Wide Web. The Internet is a massive network of networks, a networking infrastructure. It connects millions of computers together globally, forming a network in which any computer can communicate with any other computer as long as they are both connected to the Internet. The World Wide Web, or simply Web, is a way of accessing information over the medium of the Internet. It is an information-sharing model that is built on top of the Internet.

SOURCES AVAILABLE ON INTERNET

As Information Sources are broadly categories into primary, secondary and tertiary. All these three types of information sources are available on Internet. However, it is most important that all the print sources available in the world are not available via the Internet. But still, it is the one of the easiest ways to locate information. While searching the internet, it is advisable to use an effective engine like Google. For location of the primary periodicals in the internet, search can be conducted with the URL of the periodical, in case URL is not known titles or subject may be used. Sources which are available via Internet are Books, Journals, Patents, Standards, Theses and Dissertations, Research and Technical reports, Trade literature, Encyclopedias, Dictionaries Directories etc.

Books

An electronic book is commonly referred to as an e-book and is simply a print book in an electronic format. E-books can be produced in numerous formats that range from very basic text files to well structured, purpose-built files that use one of the emerging standards for e-books such as the e-Pub and Adobe PDF standards (which is covered in the section emerging standards below). As with print books, the e-book can be reference or narrative focused. A large part of the interest in e-books is that they offer a new type of user experience for reading books that provide potential benefits such as new ways to access a book catalogue and flexible choices for delivery. The potential for interactivity (e.g. hyperlinking) and the inclusion of multimedia, is where they differ from traditional print based books and is where they can possibly have the advantage to support learning and teaching. Where a print book is commonly linear and with limited features: a contents list, content and an index, an e-book is structured like a web page providing the reader with additional features that enable fast navigation through hyperlinking, annotation and keyword searches supporting multiple reader journeys through the content. It is these features that will be of interest to those thinking of building their own e-book. E-books can be delivered or accessed via a number of channels. Common delivery methods are email or download, either from a repository or e-book store. E-books are viewed using an e-book reader, which may either be traditional desktop software or by using a mobile device (including purpose-built e-readers) both of which are introduced later in this guide. It is now possible to surf the net and purchase books online. The table shows the internet bookshops and their URLs.

Sl. No.	*Internet bookshops*	*URL*
1	Indian books	http://www.indianbookshop.com
2	Worldwide Books	http://www.worldwide.com
3	Amazon.com	http://www.amazon.com
4	D.K. Agencies	http://www.dkagencies.com
5	Heritage Bookshop	http://www.heritage.books/shoping.html
6	Amazon.co.uk	http://www.amazon.co.uk
7	Blackwells.co.uk	http://www.bookshop.blackwell.co.uk

Journals

Since the seventeenth century, the printed journal has been the backbone of scholarly communication but "since the 1990s, the form of journals has been transformed into digital versions that speed both access and delivery of articles to readers and provide enhanced functionality. E-journals are now more popular with libraries and readers than their print counterparts, although both forms continue to exist for a majority of titles" (Tenopir, 2009). Scholars now have come to rely more on e-journals for communicating research ideas and results among fellow professionals. Even libraries are now providing access to more and more e-journals to boost up educational and research programmes. Access to e-Journals has definitely boosted research activities in all disciplines of study. The authorities are coming forward to support providing greater access to e-journals through one source or the other, by joining consortia or subscribing directly with the publishers. The fruits of such effort are already visible in the form of space-saving, time-saving in cataloguing and maintaining print journals etc. The only drawback that the e-journals suffer from is that most of them are not yet peer reviewed but the trend of their becoming so is on the increase. Their becoming peer reviewed will enhance their popularity and stimulate the trend of publishing in them. The future is definitely in favor of e-journals. In the field of medical Science free journals are available under http://www.freemedicaljournals.com.

Patents

A patent is an exclusive right granted by the government to the inventor to manufacture, use or seek an invention for a certain number of years. It is the right to exclude others from making, using, offering for sale or selling their invention. It is generally issued by Patent and Trademark Office. Patents are the most authentic source of information on scientific and technical development. The database can be searched through patent numbers, keywords etc. Patents are regarded as the primary source because they deal with new discoveries and inventions. The invention can be patent only if they are new. Patents are the useful source of information for researcher and scientist. Patent Search via internet;

Sl. No.	*Patent Information*	*URL*
1	US Patents full text	www.upsto.govn/patft
2	Guide to patents and patents information	www.europeanpatent-office.org/epo/online/index

Standards

A standard is a document that provides requirements, specifications, guidelines or characteristics that can be used consistently to ensure that materials, products, processes, and services are fit for their purpose. It is the primary source of information. These are very useful for researcher, scientist, engineers and industrialist. Standards are issued by certain authorities of various countries; such as Bureau of Indian Standards in India, British Standard Institution in U.K. etc. Some standards have free access while some require crossing the process of subscription.

Standards Search via internet;

Sl. No.	*Patent Information*	*URL*
1.	Bureau of Indian Standards (national standard bo y of India)	www.bis.org.in
2.	British Standards Institution (BSI)	www.bis.org.uk/
3.	International Standards	www.scilib.ucsd.edu/sbjectdir/standards

Theses and Dissertation

The term "thesis" comes from the Greek meaning "*something put forth*", and refers to an intellectual proposition. "Dissertation" comes from the Latin dissertation, meaning "*path*". These are among the important sources of information required by the researcher and scientist. As research is time-consuming and requires lot of funds so, Theses and dissertation plays vital role to carry the research without any loss. As research is the part of higher education and Research Institutes and it is not even wrong to say that the reputed institutes have excellent research and they are known for their research work only. So, many of such organization and institutions which are related with research generally created their homepage which provides the detail of theses and dissertation submitted.

Example: UMI ProQuest Dissertation (www.umi.com/dissertation)

University of Delhi, Guru Nanak Dev University, Punjab University etc have their own homepage which provides the detail of theses and dissertation submitted to the universities.

Research and Technical Reports

A research and technical report (also: scientific report) is a document that describes the process, progress, or results of technical or scientific research or the state of a technical or scientific research problem[1,2]. It might also include recommendations and conclusions of the research. Unlike other scientific literature, such as scientific journals and the proceedings of some academic conferences, technical reports rarely undergo comprehensive independent peer review before publication. They may be considered as grey literature. Where there is a review process, it is often limited to within the originating organization. Similarly, there are no formal publishing procedures for such reports, except where established locally.

Example : Networked Computer Science Technical Reports Library (www.ncrtrl.org)

Trade literature

Trade literature can be defined as promotional literature produced by, or on behalf of, manufacturers or retailers describing goods for sale. Historic examples of trade literature include trade cards, bill-heads and price lists as well as more extensive multi-paged catalogues. Current examples of trade literature can appear in a range of formats including data sheets, brochures, catalogues, loose-leaf binders, microfiche, CD-ROMs and most recently web pages. In recent years the potential for trade literature to support the study of a variety of subjects has become apparent. Trade literature is increasingly being used as primary source material in studies ranging from business history to the study of advertising techniques. Most of the organizations have their homepage which provides the important information about their product, functions services etc. There is millions of website hosted by the trade organizations.

Encyclopedias

An encyclopedia is defined as a book or set of books, optical disc, mobile device, or online informational resource containing articles on various topics, usually in alphabetical arrangement, covering all branches of knowledge or, less commonly, all aspects of one subject. These are the rich source of information. Few examples of encyclopedias available on via internet are:

- Encyclopedia.com (www.encyclopedia.com) offers millions of free articles, pictures, facts, and biographies along with information about topics like the arts, science, sports, medicine, accounting, and management. Encyclopedia.com is an ideal online reference source for researchers, students, educators, and professionals alike.
- Encyclopedia - Wikipedia, the encyclopedia (en.wiki pedia.org/wiki/ Encyclopedia) contain general articles.
- Encyclopedia Britannica: Britannica.com (www. britannica.com) Explore the updated online encyclopedia from Encyclopedia Britannica with hundreds of thousands of articles, biographies, videos, images, and Web sites.

Dictionaries

Dictionary is a book or electronic resource that lists the words of a language (typically in alphabetical order) and gives their meaning, or gives the equivalent words in a different language. A dictionary is a very important tool for anyone who is learning a new language. With a good dictionary you can do the following:

- look up the meaning of an English word you see or hear
- find the English translation of a word in your language
- check the spelling of a word
- check the plural of a noun or past tense of a verb
- find out other grammatical information about a word
- find the synonym or antonym of a word
- look up the collocations of a word
- check the part of speech of a word
- find out how to say a word
- find out about the register of a word
- find examples of the use of a word in natural language

Some dictionaries are available online free of cost .Few of are as follows:

- Dictionary.com ...dictionary.reference.com/
- Cambridge Free English Dictionary and Thesaurus
- Oxford Dictionaries - Dictionary, Thesaurus, & Grammar www.oxforddictionaries.com/
- Merriam-Webster: Dictionary and Thesaurus www.merriam-webster.com/
- Macmillan Dictionary | Free English Dictionary and... www.macmillandictionary.com

CONCLUSION

The Internet can promote better knowledge delivery/ accessibility and long-lasting knowledge repository; hence the researchers should make use of this facility to keep abreast with the e-resources technology. Educational institutions should encourage scholars in the use of e-books. They should acquire more e-books and they should have a separate e-book collection sufficient funds should be allotted to purchase the same if not freely available. Free facilities should be provided to the researchers to view the e-books. The printed book will not disappear overnight. Continuing trend in the balance between print and e-books will definitely support the increasing number of researchers in various disciplines particulars in the University sector.

REFERENCES

1 Herring, M Y (2001) Ten reasons why the Internet is not substitute for a library", *American Libraries*, April. pp76-78.

2 KT, Dili (2009) *Library and information science in digital era*, Atlantic, New Delhi, Atlantic.

3 Vasanthi, M Christina (2001) The changing environment of academic libraries: end user education and planning strategies for libraries in India, *Library Philosophy and Practice*, 4(1)

4 Rao, N L and Prasanna, M K, (2001) Use of Internet for Improving library services", *SRELS Journal of Information Management*. 38(1) pp15-30

5 Rudenstine, N L (1996) *The Internet and higher education*, Harvard Conference on the Internet and society, 29-31 May

6 Saeed H et al, "Internet use in university libraries of Pakistan" online information reviews 24(2) (2000) 154 to160

7 Sandy Berger's Great Age Guide to the Internet By Sandy Berger. Que Publishing, 2005.

8 Vignesh, SN (2009), 'The future scenario of digital library era', SRELS Journal of Information Management, vol.46, no.1, pp. 25-28.

2

Usability Analysis of Academic Library Websites: A Conceptual Approach

Nitesh Kumar Verma
Assistant Librarian
Babasaheb Bhimrao Ambedkar University, Lucknow, U.P.
Akhandanand Shukla
Assistant Professor
Mizoram University, Aizawl, Mizoram

ABSTRACT

The influence of ICT in developing countries demands more web-based services, and nowadays it is very easy to visit any website to seek any information from them. The library websites are the main gateway to their knowledge which makes a library to reach remote users and provide their services effectively and efficiently at their fingertips. It is very necessary to carry out the usability analysis of the library websites to know how usable they are to cope, users, demands, and needs. The present paper briefly describes the library usability analysis, its attributes, how to do it? Discuss the methods of usability analysis and advantages.

Keywords : Library Website, Website Usability, Website evaluation, Content Analysis

INTRODUCTION

The World Wide Web (WWW) is used to access the huge quantity of information available through the Internet and become the largest source of information for academic and research activities. To cope up the growing demand of users for information exchange, the easiest and effective way is websites. In the recent years, websites play a vital role through which information is disseminated effectively and efficiently. A website is a collection of multiple webpages, images, videos or other electronic objects that are linked together with a common Uniform Resource Locator (URL) and collectively it is hosted on a web server computer accessible via networks such as the Internet or local area network. The web services, rendered through websites have been gathering significant momentum in both academia and industry in the recent years.

An academic organization's website is the main gateway to its information, products, and services. It should be a reflection of the needs of its users which it serves. Unfortunately, website design is often driven by technology, organizational structure or business objectives, rather than by users needs. Library websites are also selected frequently to obtain scholarly and educational resources in academia. A library website plays a role of an extension and amplification of a traditional library and offers a range of library services such as electronic resource access, online catalogues (OPAC) and online reference services. As many libraries move forward into the digital age, web presence becomes increasingly important for meeting the needs of users. As the academic library website serves as a key gateway to library services, usability analysis and evaluation of libraries website is paramount. While there is much coverage of usability analysis and assessment of academic libraries website because libraries website is taking more attention to serving primary sources of information for their users; and for many services and sources, library users depend on the library websites.

LIBRARY WEBSITES

The library websites are the primary source of all the information to their hosting institutions or organizations. A university website is increasingly used for the variety of purposes like attracting new students, information regarding courses, syllabus, job vacancies, the library catalogue, acts as a centre place for news and announcements. The library websites have to serve various categories of students and researchers who are looking for reliable, relevant and quality information. Students need information for studying, achieving the academic purpose and doing assignments. Researchers need information for their research and new information or knowledge. Since web portals are an integral part of the institutions, it also provides direct access to library and their digital resources.

The accessibility of information in the digital formats in libraries and information centres and other agencies has made easier and quicker access to the desired information because of increasing web graphics and interactive capabilities which allow their users to search, store, and disseminate information. Full-text articles which include texts, graphs, images, tables, etc. which results in all type of organization recognize the importance of Internet and websites not only for dissemination of information but also as a medium for popularizing their activities, products, and services.

Therefore, the educational library websites should structure and organize quality content and information. On the other hand, the quality and diversity of information and many other factors affecting information seeking on library websites which affect students and researchers when accessing information. If a good library may have an outdated website that turns a user off. Different libraries have different target groups, various types of services, resources, etc. which depends on their host institution. The efforts are made by inside experts or any outside agency to update the websites regularly. The contents and information available on the website are also not up to the mark.

USABILITY ANALYSIS

The term usability was mostly used in between 1980's, and there are many approaches to making a product or services usable, and no accepted definition of the term usability. Usability is how easy an item is to use, and the item can be anything. In the case of websites, usability has been defined as the effortlessness at which a normal person can use the website to achieve their objectives. Usability is comprised of 5 things i.e. learnability, memorability, efficiency, satisfaction, and errors.

Basic Usability Attributes

It is both quantitative and qualitative measurement of the design of a website user interface, grouped into five broad factors based on Nielson's (1993) five attributes. These are discussed as follows:

Learnability

Learnability has to do with how easily users can begin to do productive work with a system, which is new for them. Ease of learning is another wording for this usability attribute, as it is mentioned by most sources (Dix, Abowd, Beale, & Finalay, 1993; Nielsen, 1993; Shneiderman, 1998). Learnability is how quickly and easily users can reach a level of proficiency in using the system (website).

Efficiency

Nielsen (1993) defines efficiency refers to an expert user's steady-state level of Performance at the time when the learning curve flattens out. Dix et al. (1993) and Wixon (1997) specified efficiency as long-term performance, therefore associating it somehow with expert users as well. Efficiency is the number of tasks per unit of time that the user can perform using the system.

Memorability

This refers to the ease of remembering the way a system must be operated. Nielsen (1993) describes this as the characteristic of a system that allows the user to return to the system after some period not having used it, without having to learn everything all over again.

Error rate

This refers to the errors made during the utilization of the system and how easy it is to recover from them. According to Shneiderman (1998) and Nielsen (1993), errors can have an impact on efficiency, by slowing down performance.

Satisfaction

It is the subjective opinion that users from the system (or about some parts of it). It is the most elusive usability attribute, as it is entirely dependent on the subjective opinion of users.

WEBSITE USABILITY ANALYSIS

Website usability is a technique which refers to methods for improving ease-of-use during the design process (Nielsen, 2003). The International Organization for Standardization (ISO) defines usability of a product as "the extent to which the product can be used by specific users to achieve specified goals with 'effectiveness,' 'efficiency' and 'satisfaction' in a specified context of use." According to Nielsen (1999) "with the fast development and increasing use of the World Wide Web as both information-seeking and an electronic commerce tool, web user interface studies grow in significance. Poor interface functionality is one potential cause for web usability meltdown." Three of the views relates to how usability should be measured:

- The product-oriented view: It can be measured regarding the ergonomic attributes of the product;
- The user-oriented view: It can be measured regarding the mental effort and attitude of the user;
- The user performance view: It can be measured by examining how the user interacts with the product, with particular emphasis on either ease-of-use or

acceptability in the real world.

There are many things to consider for building a new website. The website needs to be attractive enough that people want to look at it. It also needs to contain all of the information that a person wants to share with their readers to help them achieve the objective for which they came to the website. One of the most important aspects of building a website is testing for usability. Users visit websites and also return to previously accessed sites if they easily find useful information, organized and presented according to a well-structured layout. Acceptability of Web applications by users strictly relies on their usability. Usability is one significant factor of the quality of Web applications. If usability is more than the quality of that website, its implementation will be more. In recent times, it has been receiving significant attention, being recognized as elementary assets for the success of websites. Searching new methods for ensuring usability is, one of the current objectives of the website's research and much more attention on usability is currently paid by industry, which is recognizing the importance of adopting usability methods, for verifying the usability of Web applications before and after their deployment. Libraries have recognized the potential of WWW by developing innovative ways to meet users' needs, in a digital academic culture, by essentially designing user-friendly websites.

HOW WEBSITE USABILITY IS DIFFERING FROM WEBSITE CONTENT ANALYSIS?

Website content analysis is a systematic technique for coding symbolic content (text, images, audio, video, etc.) found on particular web pages, especially structural features (Bauer, 2000). In website content analysis, contents of the particular website e.g. website images, texts, audio files, pdf files, video files, websites' services, etc. have been measured and evaluated whereas in usability analysis understandability, learnability, operability, funcationalibility, credibility, layout & design quality, information architecture, etc. have been measured and evaluated.

WHY WEBSITE USABILITY IS IMPORTANT?

The main reason of website usability is so important that there are so many common websites, if users found a particular website not usable they will go to another website. If a particular website is a most attractive website in the world, but people will leave immediately if they are unable to navigate the website easily. As mentioned in the article "Why Web Site Usability is Important for an Organization," on the web, big institutions fully rely on their web existence to achieve their online goals. Similarly, a user will judge the organization as good as their website is.

Besides that, good websites increase user satisfaction whereas websites which violate usability guidelines confuse users and result in a loss of users and revenue for the institution behind them. This is because increasing usability is a good way to attract users to visit the website. Useful websites that are easy to use bring in users and give a particular site a competitive edge over the competition.

METHODS TO CALCULATE USABILITY

There are different methods for testing usability; some popular methods are as follows:

Studies to record participant's comments

While making the usability testing observations of the participant's comments should be recorded. This can be done by two approaches – think-aloud and retrospective. When using the "think aloud" method, users report on the incidents that they happen. While using the retrospective approach, users perform all tasks uninterrupted, and then watch their session video and report any observations.

Eye tracking studies

It is the process of measuring either the point of gaze (where one is looking) or the motion of an eye. Eye trackers provide options for analyzing the data in different ways. By generating the heat maps and eye gaze plot, eye-tracking results can be graphically analyzed.

The online survey, email feedback

Usability testing for a website could also be done by creating a questionnaire for online surveys or by asking the website users to give feedback on the website.

Heuristic evaluation method

This is one of the usability inspection methods, where the User Interface is judged against compliance with well-recognized usability principles (which are heuristic basically).

Testing by usability experts

Usually, two to five usability experts could be employed for finding the usability issues with the interface.

Inspection evaluation–cognitive walkthrough

Cognitive walkthrough for the web is a usability inspection evaluation method where participants are not needed for the testing purpose. There are different Cognitive models which simulate web-navigation and could be used for finding usability problems of the website.

As above there are various methods that could be used for web usability testing. However, opting for a single usability method may not identify all usability problems. According to the study by Jan Horsky et al. the methods for usability evaluation of email response, online survey, observations, and interviews are complementary, i.e., each of them characterizes a different usability aspect, and no single method identifies all or most problems.

BASIC CATEGORIES FOR USABILITY TESTING

Broadly website usability testing may be categorized into ten further categories to know or evaluate the usability of a particular website. These ten categories include:

- Content relevance
- Ease of use and decision-making
- Graphics
- Interactivity between the site and the user
- Interface design
- Links
- Navigation/Menus
- Page layout/Text formatting
- Search tools
- Technical performance

Nielsen (1994) in their earlier study earlier presented in separate tables, for web usability and also divided the web usability checklists into some heads.

Table 1. Nielsen's (1994) Categories for Use in Heuristic Evaluations

Sl. No.	*Category*	*Description*
1.	Visibility of System Status	Provide feedback, indicate progress, identify cues, etc
2.	Match between system and real world	Speak tl e users, language, familiar terms, etc.
3.	User control & freedom	The obvious way to undo, make actions reversible, etc.
4.	Consistency and standards	Express same thing the same way, uniformity, etc.
5.	Error prevention	Design system to prevent errors identify cues, etc.
6.	Recognition rather than recall	See and point instead of remembering and tell, etc.
7.	Flexibility and efficiency of use	User interface customizable, shortcuts, etc.
8.	Aesthetic and Minimalist design	Straightforward and attractive design.
9.	Helping and recovering	Assisting users, recognize, diagnose and recover from the errors

Chiou, Lin, and Perng's (2012) identify categories to test website usability. Over 83 journal articles were reviewed to identify 53 criteria for website usability testing; these criteria are consolidated into twelve categories.

Table 2. Chiou et al. (2010)
12 Categories of Website Usability Testing

Sl. No.	*Category*	*Descriptions*
1.	Ease of Use	Usability, accessibility, navigability, and logical structure
2.	Responsiveness	Accessibility of services, e-mail service, reply to users, contact information, and intuitive online help
3.	Fulfilment	Online working services, availability of necessary information
4.	Security/Privacy	Information protection and privacy statement policy
5.	Personalization	Individualized attention, customization of offering and information.
6.	Visual Appearances	Attract attention, convey image, and aesthetics
7.	Trust	Name reorganization, consistency, intention and credibility
8.	Interactivity	Interactive features and communication (FAQ, Chats, etc)
9.	Advertising/ Persuasion	Marketing of information, promotion of services, suggested information, etc.
10.	Playfulness	Enjoyment, fun, pleasure, and flow
11.	Technology integration	New technology and its integration
12.	Information and services quality	Variety, scope, conciseness, accuracy, authority, reliability and uniqueness.

ADVANTAGES' OF WEB USABILITY ANALYSIS

As noted by Hallahan (2001), Usability experts suggest a variety of reasons for conducting usability tests. This includes:

- The assurance of ease [of use] and satisfaction by users,
- Saves users time,
- Establishment of benchmarks for future versions design and developments,
- Improve the page load time, accuracy and updated,
- Minimization of service, training, and support costs,
- Increased use and support of the site by users,
- Imperative to be competitive.

Levi and Conrad (2008) explain that the website development lifecycle is the same as that used for traditional software, including requirement gathering, analysis, design, implementation, testing and deployment, "and that just as traditional software development should have a functionality and usability component, so should Web development efforts.

CONCLUSION

The increasing use of Internet has changed the method of accessing, disseminating information about library activities, services, rules and regulations, admissions, various sections, staff, etc. The library webpages of academic institutions not only serve as a great platform for publishing the library news, activities, programs, resources and services but it also helps to disseminate the important notice to all the remote user. The information furnished in the websites of Libraries need to be evaluated and analyzed periodically using recognized criteria like web design, accessibility, arrangement, etc. This will help the universities to improve their websites usability, accessibility as per their user's needs. Usability is the key aspect of user-centred internet sites. Usability is considered as a personal quality attribute of the system (Folmer and Bosch, 2004). From the available literature, it is found that the usability depends upon the perceptions of the individual user and there are not any established criteria for its evaluation. To maintain the standard, design and structure of Indian academic library websites it is highly recommended for regular assessment of these library web portals to increase their usability and accessibility.

REFERENCES

1. Abdullah, A. (2001). A comparative study of academic libraries websites in Malaysia. Retrieved from http://ir.uitm.edu.my/27/
2. Agarwal R. and Venkatesh V. (2002). Assessing a Firm's Web Presence: A Heuristic Evaluation Procedure for the Measurement of Usability. Information Systems Research, 13(2), 168–186.
3. Aziz, N. S., Kamaludin, A., & Sulaiman, N. (2013). Assessing website usability measurement. International Journal of Research in Engineering and Technology, 2(9), 386-392.
4. Bauer, M. (2000). Classical content analysis: A Review. Qualitative researching with text, image, and sound: A practical handbook (pp. 131-151). London: Sage.
5. Chiew K. T. and Salim S. S. (2003). WEBUSE: Website Usability Evaluation Tools, University of Malaya.
6. Corry D., Frick W. and Hansen L. (1997). User Centred Design and Usability Testing of a Web Site: An Illustrative Case Study, Educational Technology, Research & Development.
7. Ebenezer, Catherine (2003). Usability evaluation of an NHS library website. Health Information and Libraries Journal. 134-142.
8. Ivory, M.Y. & Hearst, M.A. (2002). The state of the art in automating Usability evaluation of user Interfaces. ACM computing surveys, 33(4), 56-63.
9. Jasek, C. (2007). How to Design Library Websites to Maximize Usability. Library Connect.
10. Mohamadesmaeil, Sedigheh & Koohbanani, Somaye Kazemi (2013). Web usability evaluation of Iran National Library website. Collnet Journal of Scientometrics and Information Management, 6 (1), 1-14.
11. Mustafa, S. & Al-Zoua'bi, L. (2008). Usability of the academic websites of Jordan's universities: an evaluative study, The International Arab Conference on Information Technology, Tunisia.
12. Nielsen J. (2006). Usability 101: Introduction to usability. Retrieved 2 November 2016, from http://www.useit.com/alertbox/20030825.html

13. Nielsen, J. (1999). Voodoo usability. Alterbox. Retrieved 2 -November 2016 from http://www.useit.com/alertbox/991212.html

14. Nielsen, J. (2001). How to conduct a heuristic evaluation. Available at www.useit.com/papers/heuristic

15. Nielsen, J. (2003). Usability 101: Introduction to usability. Alertbox. Retrieved 2 November 2016, from http://www.useit.com/alertbox/20030825.html

16. Pearson J., Pearson A., and Green D. (2007). Determining the Importance of Key Criteria in Web Usability. Management Research News, 30(11), 816-828.

17. Ramesh Babu, B., Narendra Kumar, A. M. & Gopalkrishnan, S. (2009). Credibility of university websites in Tamil Nadu, DESIDOC Journal of Library & Information Technology. 29(3), 16-28.

18. Shrivastava, R., Pandey, R. K. & Kumar, M. (2012). Ranking of academic websites on the basis of external quality measurement. Journal of emerging trends in cmputing and information science, 3(4), 547-553.

19. Smith, M., Rougier, B., Hamman, D., McKenzi, J., Johnston, B. and Maylath, B. (2001). Website Usability Evaluation of www.uwstout.edu", The University of Wisconsin-Stouta, Website Usability Testing Centre.

20. Tarafdar, M., & Zhang, J. (2005). Analyzing the Influence of Website Design Parameters on Website Usability. Information Resources Management Journal, 18(4), 62-80.

21. Tobin, T., & Kesselman, M. (2000). Evaluation of web-based library instruction programs. Inspel, 34(2), 67-75.

22. Vasanth Raju, N. & Harinarayana, N. S. (2008). An analysis of usability features of library websites. Annals of Library and Information Studies, 111-122.

23. Yusuf, M. A. (2014). Usability evaluation of university library websites based on students preferences. Australian Journal of Basic and Applied Sciences, 98-111.

24. Horsky, J., McColgan, K., Pang, J. E., Melnikas, A. J., Linder, J. A., Schnipper, J. L., and Middleton, B. Complementary methods of system usability evaluation: Surveys and observations during software design and development cycles, Journal of Biomedical Informatics 43 (2010), 782–790.

25. Chiou, W-C., Lin, C-C., & Perng, C. (2010). A strategic framework

for website evaluation based on a review of the literature from 1995–2006. Information & Management, 47(5–6), 282– 290.

26. Devi, Krishna Ksh and Verma, Manoj Kumar (2016). Conceptual Approach of Web Content Analysis: A Tool to Analyses Library Website to Improve their Web Based Services in Academic Institutions. in International Conference Proceeding on-Contemporary Innovations in Library Information Science, Social Science and Technology for Virtual World (pp. 132-138), New Delhi.

3

Role of Mobile Technology and their Application in Library Services in Digital Era

Karan Singh

Ph. D. Scholar, Sambalpur University, Odisha

ABSTRACT

This paper is focusing on the potential of mobile devices in Library and Information centres. Implementation of mobile Technology has changed the way of people to access and communicate information. Users want easy and instant access to relevant information, putting pressure on Library and Information Science (LIS) professionals to think out of the box for meeting their information needs. Application of mobile phones to provide library and information services is a significant step in this direction. In this 21st century Library and information science professional's essential to use mobile technology in libraries and this new technology offering outreach technical options for librarians. Libraries have the well opportunity to extend new different types of library services to users. This study is a new platform for reaching students and staff members. The main purpose of this study mobile technology use in higher education generally and particularly effective utilize in libraries and library services.

Keywords : Mobile technology, Library science, Digital India, Services, Information and communication

INTRODUCTION

Today access information is has become vital. Now a day mobile phone is a part of human life without it life may not survive. Mobile technology is playing very significant role in user's information seeking behaviour in such a way teaching, learning and research work as per users need. It is model of nanotechnology. Now 371 mm of people use Mobile for various purposes. Child to old man and rural to urban everybody use mobile technology access. To library resources it is not a new concept; in fact, the first project designed to deliver handheld mobile access to library patrons began eighteen years ago, in 1993, the time of mainframe computers and Gopher. Now the Android mobile users can gathere their information, store, organize, accesse, retrieve and consume. A growing number of users are engaging mobile phone as search tools. Smart Phones cell phones, i-phones, and tablets are now common among the first places people turn when seeking information.

Mobile must play a key role in enabling Digital India, In India, talk about Digital India and Smart Cities is quite the rage. Connected mobile devices can now connect people and things almost anywhere and anytime. This makes the customer a 24/7 phenomenon, reachable at any time and who can transact at any moment, infinitely broadening the opportunity as well as the threat from competition. With access to applications which reside on the cloud, almost every mobile device with internet access today has access to a huge amount of computing power. Mobile phones have revolutionized the daily lives of ordinary people. Mobile phones (also called cellular phone or cell phone) do not use wires or cables, but work with radio waves and can be carried about and used anywhere (Homby, 2001). Mobile phones are currently being used successfully in India and in other developing countries to share information in the areas of research, teaching, learning, health, agriculture, etc.

BRIEF HISTORY OF MOBILE PHONES/GSM IN INDIA

GSM world (2004) explains that GSM supports more advanced data technologies. These technologies allow for a greater bandwidth and permit the development of mobile applications. According to Aragba-Akpore (2003), "GSM dominates the world today. As the most matured digital-cellular standard, GSM networks offer cellular switched data services well in advance of other networks." GSM is known as the second generations (2G) after the old analogue system, which was first generation (1G). The advent of GSM was revolutionary, especially because of its roaming capabilities. (Iwhiwhu, 2010)

Telecommunication services were introduced in India by the British Colonial Government in 1886 to facilitate colonial administration in the country. After independence, in 1966, there were only 18,724 telephone lines for use by a population of about 40 million people (Edison, 2002). In January 1985, the Post and Telecommunications Department split into a postal division and a telecommunication division. The latter was merged with the Nigerian External Telecommunication Limited (NITEL). Its main objective is to harmonize the planning and coordination of the internal and external telecommunications services (Edison, 2002). Two mobile cellular telephone networks were approved in September, 1997 by the Ministry of Communication and The Indian Telecommunications limited (ITEL) cellular network and mobile Telecommunications services Limited (MTS), managed by NITEL cover Lagos, Enugu, and Abuja with a capacity of 10,000 lines having one mobile switching centre (MSC) in each area, while MTS Ltd. operates 5,000 cellular line capacity network based in Victoria Island, Lagos (Ndukwe, 2003).

ROLE MOBILE IN DIGITAL INDIA

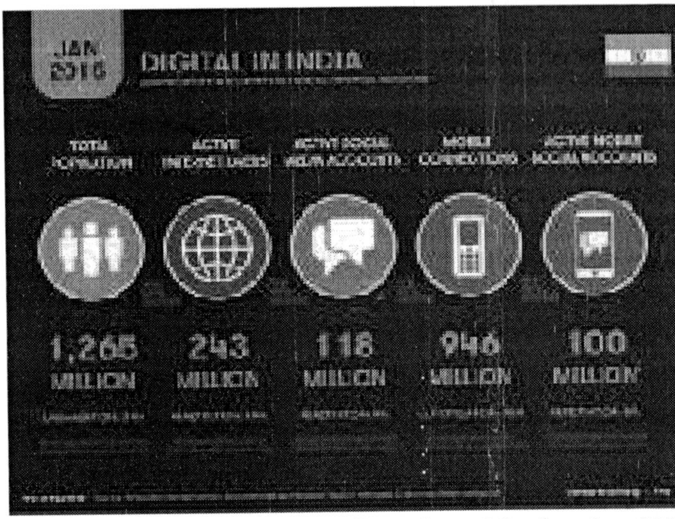

https://www.techinasia.com/india-web-mobile-data-jan-2015

According to 'Digitalinsights' Indians are very dynamic because 946 Million peoples are connected Mobile connections and 100 million activated mobiles through social accounts. Mobile phones are more frequent and are increasingly starting to look like computers and a number of different phones are include messaging platform (Davis, 2012). Mobile phone is most effective communication tool device it has undergone several changes to make its functionalities exceeding the traditional voice communication among two persons (Kushchu, 2007). Mobile technologies are new communication tools and these are transforming how people can search the information, receive the information and interact with the information on everyday basis. These mobile phone tools offer convenient access to the world information, across borders of subject, discipline and organization. In present day developed countries are using lack of access to the affordable Internet. In recognition of this role, grants and policy initiatives around the world have targeted libraries as a community resource that can provide access to and sustain the informational resources presented by the Internet. (Thompson et al., 2014)

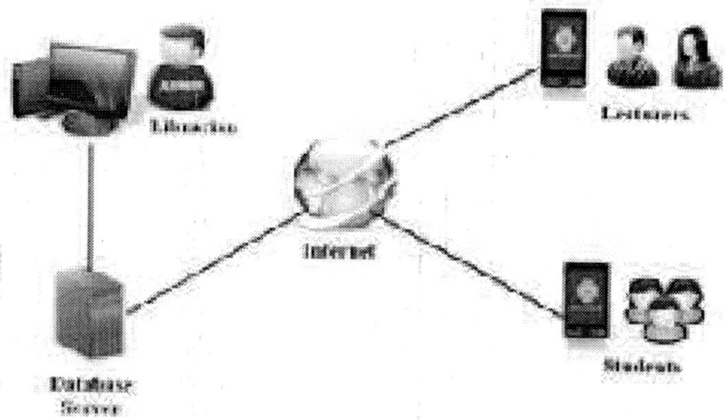

In Fig. 2 indicates that all data stored on the server information. Administrator or librarian can manage data information that will happen in the library service. Lecturers and students can receive information through mobile library applications.

List of few mobile technology use in libraries and information centres

Sl. No.	*Name of the Library*	*Description*	*URL Address*
1	The New York Public Library	It provides online public access Catalogue (OPACs) and databases.	http://m.nypl.org
2	Adelphi University Libraries Mobile	Offers library staff members contact information, library timings and a link to the library blog etc...	http://m.adelphi.edu/library/
3	Duke University	This university produced a free iPhone application called DukeMobile, containing information on digital library resources.	http://itunes.apple.com/app/dukemobile/id306796270?mt=8

4	Albertsons Library, Boise State University	It offers simple text navigation and it provides library details ex: study room, computer sections, Book call numbers shelving list etc...	http://library.boisestate.edu/m
5	East Carolina University	This university provides library instructional materials and resources via mobile phones	www.ecu.edu/cs-dhs/laupuslibrary/researchfirstaid.cfm
6	Virginia Tech University Library	It offers library timings, library catalogue search and library location etc..	http://m.lib.vt.edu/
7	North Carolina State University Library	This university effective layout provides group finders and the main feature is to view the number of available computers in the library for the students.	http://lib.ncsu.edu/m/home/?browse=iphone
8	PENN Libraries, University of Pennsylvania	This university offer users to search databases, library video clips etc..., information's are provided.	http://www.library.upenn.edu/m/
9	Worldcat	It offers library catalogue search with author wise and Hiremate, 2015	http://worldcat mobile.org

MOBILE PHONES AND LIBRARY SERVICES

ICT has collapsed barriers and promoted fast

communication and interactions across boundaries. The need to meet life's basic challenges and responsibilities has informed the invention and the use of information technologies (Ademodi and Adepoju, 2009). Libraries are deeply interested in channels for the transmission of information, such as telephones and telephone lines, cellular networks, cable television, and the Internet. Academic libraries are challenged in satisfying their customer's needs since their target market (researchers, lecturers, undergraduate, and postgraduate students) is demanding and dynamic. The Internet and World Wide Web (www) have made it possible for university teachers, researchers, and students to locate what they need without going to the library. If librarians in this sector are to continue to make substantial contributions as information disseminators, they will have to understand and exploit ICT infrastructure and emerging technologies in delivering services to their clientele (Ikhemuemhe, 2005).

According to Terplan (2000), "telephones and e-mail are important tools to facilitate prompt handling and response to the stream of patron questions from within and out of the library user community. Most university libraries have one phone line, which is mostly used for administrative purposes and located in the library administrator's office. Mobile phones could be deployed at the enquiring desks." Short Message Services (SMS) or text facilities available on all mobile phones, could be used to create awareness amongst the academic library clientele about upcoming events and new arrivals. This could be flashed through a facility called "broadcast" where one text message is sent to all the library contacts listed in the address book on the mobile phone at once.

Academic libraries need to keep abreast of the dynamically changing needs of their clientele. One way of delivering user-centred services is library surveys. Surveys could be carried with text and multimedia messaging. Patrons could text a coded number to a particular phone line to indicate their preference. Specialized and personalized information services can be achieved using the wireless technologies made available to all.

MOBILE TECHNOLOGIES AND LIBRARY SERVICES

In the Teaching and learning, mobile technology can be very efficiently used. As the strength of libraries is in supporting self-directed and independent learning, libraries could play an increasingly important role in this mode of learning libraries could provide access to resources. A list of possible mobile service is listed below:

- Mobile library site
- Mobile Online Public Access Catalogue (MOPAC)
- Circulation services
- Reference Enquiry services
- Current Awareness Service and Selective Dissemination of Information Service (CAS & SDI)
- E-mail and SMS –Service
- Distribution of E-Resources through Mobile site
- Library Maps and floor plans
- Library News, Events and Blogs
- Library Hours and library tours
- Mobile databases
- Inter library loan service
- List of new Arrivals
- Books and Article's search
- Mobile apps for library
- Library instructional program through mobile site
- Subject guide, path-finders etc.
- Photo/Video gallery
- Library Surveys
- SMS Services

- Feedback/Comments/Suggestions
- Contacting library staff for help
- Mobile database - PubMed for Handhelds is a mobile web portal for the National Library of Medicine.

Mobile devices can be enabled to use a variety of communication technologies such as:

- Wi-Fi (wireless fidelity): It is a type of wireless local area network technology.
- Bluetooth: It connects mobile devices wirelessly.
- 3G (Third Generation): Global system for mobile communication (GSM) and general packet radio service (GPRS).
- Data services: data networking services for mobile phones
- Dial-up services: Data networking services for mobile phones. Mobile technology extends computing the internet into the wireless medium, and provides greater flexibility in communication, collaboration, and information sharing VPN (Virtual Private Networks) Secure access to a private network. Conversely, this technology provides unique learning opportunities and has the advantage of portability and mobility academic, public and special libraries could use mobile technology in service innovations, m-learning, instruction in mobile device, web lectures, reference service and catalogue searching.

ADVANTAGES

- It is user-friendly
- It is a personalized service
- Ability to Access Information
- Time-Saving
- User Participation
- Location Awareness

- Limitless Access

LIMITATIONS/BARRIERS

Although mobile Technology holds great promise for library services, there are some limitations or barriers in providing library services such as

- Content ownership and licensing,
- usually expensive and resource intensive
- limited memory of mobile devices
- digital rights management,
- Access to information in the digital age.
- Reach of an external vendor into the digital collections and technologies – sustained access will be an extremely important issue for libraries if they adopt mobile Library technology and services that offer content from providers outside of the library.
- Another pressing concern about mobile technology in the library is privacy - because of the risk that patron usage information can be used and exploited by law enforcement officers and those who commit identity theft. Mobile technology is changing the relationship between libraries and their users by expanding services and posing new challenges to reader's privacy.
- Issues related to trust and security - Libraries should be wary of entrusting user information to locations in the cloud that may offer a different level of protection from that provided by in-house library infrastructure
- Some of the digital content can only be accessed on certain devices, and this can have a "chilling effect" on learning and library service because it locks some people out.
- Lack of appropriate mobile-friendly academic content to meet learners' needs.
- Difficulty in supplying content to an increasingly mobile student body

- Problems in finding and accessing the content needed for mobile learners from the Library perspective
- The use of wireless devices is increasing rapidly, yet there is a concern in the scientific community that this technology could have adverse side effects.
- Lack of staff awareness and familiarity- Setting up text alerts, for instance, requires technical expertise from staff who understand how the library management system produces notifications, as well as staff or consultants who can help to set up an interface with a Sim card modem or a suitable service in order to deliver those notifications as text alerts
- the dearth of technological expertise among staff members and
- increasing staff reductions and other cutbacks

Mobile phones are still viewed by the majority of people as devices for making phone calls and text messages, so they often don't associate them with other activities, such as information seeking. However, people are increasingly dependent on their mobile phones and there is a growing minority who do use them as diaries, for taking notes and for e-mail and internet access. As a result, there may be an increase in expectation from Library users that libraries will provide some services in a mobile-friendly way

SOLUTIONS

Libraries should conduct analyses and make smart decisions, such as –

- support staff education,
- explore partnerships
- new funding models,
- Ready to compromise when it comes to their traditional information delivery models.
- Protect themselves from deceptive content agreements with third party-providers.

- need the expert knowledge of mobile devices to flow through the profession and not just lie in the hands of recent library school graduates
- tell users about the thousands of free mobile-ready books available from such initiatives as Project Gutenberg
- create opportunities to educate staff, build local expertise, and promote discussion by offering training sessions and professional development options
- Build a solid foundation of knowledge about mobile services within the organization.
- Host lectures or discussion groups or include such information in their websites, blogs, or newsletters.

CONCLUSION

Mobile technology is the essential tool for today's life and we can use to provide library services to users and through the mobile user can easily access the e-book. In future we can use Mobile phone-a-Librarian is part of 'Ask A Librarian' service that provide the information for users to get quick help in finding information on library services and resources in India also. Mobile phones are inevitable tools for information communication. The dissemination of processed information is a common factor in a civilized society. Libraries especially use several tools and techniques to circulate the information to the user community. At the same time, libraries should be advertised. For this purpose, the use of technology is very essential. Mobile technology has become boon to the libraries. A library may reach the remote users effectively by adopting of mobile technology in its services.

REFERENCES

1. Ademodi, D. T., & E. O. Adepoju (2009). Computer skill among librarians in academic libraries in Ondo and Ekiti States, Nigeria. Library Philosophy and Practice, Available: http://unllib.unl.edu/LPP/ademodi-adepoju.htm

2. Davis, M.R. (2012). AFRICA: mobile devices address equity issues. Education Week, 31(19), 6-8.

3. Hiremath, B. K. and Anand, Kenchakkanavar(2015). Mobile technology based information services in the digital world. International Journal Of Development Research ,5 (09), 5474-5477,

4. Ikhemuemhe, G. (2005). MTN Connects UNILAG with virtual library. Vanguard Newspaper 33.

5. Iwhiwhu, Basil Enemute, Ruteyan, Josiah Oghenero; and Eghwubare, Aroghene, (2010). Mobile Phones for Library Services: Prospects for Delta State University Library, Abraka. Library Philosophy and Practice (e-journal), 346.

6. Kushchu, I. (2007). Positive contributions of mobile phones to society, available at: http://www.kiwanja.net/ database/ document/report_positive_impact.pdf

7. Ndukwe, E. (2003). Mobile phones. Availabe: http:// www.unesco.org/Risi/nisicountry–profiles/Nigeria.

8. Terplan, K. (Ed.) (2000). The telecommunications handbook. Boca Raton: CRC Press

9. Thompson, K.M., Jaeger, P.T. and Taylor, N.G. (2014). Digital Literacy and Digital Inclusion: Information Policy and the Public Library, Rowman & Littlefield Publishers, Lanham, MD. 144-145 DOI:10.1080/1941126X.2015.1029789.

10. https://www.techinasia.com/india-web-mobile-data-jan-2015

4

Usage of Library Resources and Services in University Libraries : A Social Media Perspective

Rushmanasab Gurikar
Junior Research Fellow
Dept. of Library and Information Science
Karnatak University, Dharwad, Karnatak

ABSTRACT

The study intended to find the possible of utility of social media in the Indian universities. The data collected from the forty six central universities, to know what extensively social media are used, based on the popularity and specialised applications of social media are collected, used by different universities. The study explained some of social media and its application in the libraries, which are the means to provide services to the clientele. As these days social media are used widely by students and young adults in internet era.

Keywords : Resource Sharing, Library Service, Library Consortium, Library Networking, Social media, SNS.

INTRODUCTION

Academic libraries are always mainstream supporter of academic activities like teaching, learning and research.

Academic libraries are indeed providing the value-added services by extent availability of its resources. Unfortunately, many of the resources are not utilised properly and many times the availability of resources does not connect to access and usage. In order to equate the access and use, library professionals are working hard to reach out their users. Despite, their roller coaster efforts, financial barrier is restricting them. To overcome from these barrier library professionals started library co-operation between them. Gradually, this technique evolved in the library field and since, it is ever changing in its shape in the changing environment and took new dimensions. Library resource sharing is the exchange of information, document or material between the two or more treaties on some set of agreements. Earlier library resource was used to share physically, however, in the changing environment, availability of digital source and ICT facilities enables us to provide improved resources sharing technique. The birth of internet escalates the resources sharing via library networks and consortium. Today, it is possible to access any shared information from home itself, Internet made possible to access information from any corner of the world. Social media are internet based applications, through this information can be shared successfully and timely.

OBJECTIVES

- To understand the changing nature of resources sharing in libraries;
- To know the different social media and its utilities;
- To explore the possible application of social media in libraries

METHODOLOGY

The forty six central universities recognised by UGC website selected for the study. The individual university websites browsed for collecting information on the usage of social media. The names of the individual university also search in Google if any social media are used and not linked to their website. The extensive literature survey also conducted to collect the related information on using library resources and services possible via social media to identify the possible applications.

GENESIS OF RESOURCE SHARING AND NETWORKING

Store House

Initially, libraries were meant for preservation of knowledge. Those libraries were not allowed the public to access the stored information. In those days documents were only for chosen few like scholars, royal families, courtesans, etc. even many a times documents were chained. At that time, libraries were meant for storage and preserving house of knowledge.

Library Co-operation

Adequate organisations, institutions and research laboratories were started the co-operative venture between them in the 19th and 20th century. That was an urgent situation created between them due to increase of research and development activities were undertaken. The users were started demanding specialised information, but the specialised information availed with only a few organisations. To fulfil the increasing and specialised demands of the users, the libraries were started co-operating between them. Through that, both the parties could get shared information and increase their research output.

Inter Library Loan

Inter library loan is an outcome of an agreement between two parties. It also a type of service provided to the other library on demand. The target library can borrow the book or photocopy information source from the source library. Interlibrary loan helpful even today, through this a library can save money, at the same time it also accesses the unavailable information with them or in the market.

Interlibrary Loan is more effective among local library. Interlibrary loan can also process through computers; ISO developed the standard [ISO 10160 and ISO 10161] for it. OCLC is using this method by VDX and world share management system. Journals articles, documents, some time skilled professionals are popular sources shared through interlibrary loan.

Library Networks

Internet technology is made possible to access information via networks. National programme document (1975) defines that library network is two or more library involved in a common pattern of information interchange between the agreed parties. For the purpose of access the information and sharing, they use information communication technology.

The major purposes of library networking are to promote library co-operation and resource sharing among libraries, to make the best use of resources or services of libraries. So that, they can develop efficient collection development policies to reduce unnecessary redundancy wherever is possible. Some of the library networks include DELNET, INFLIBNET, MANLIBNET, ADINET, ERNET, CALIBNET, etc.

Library Consortium

A library consortium is an act of sharing information between two or more parties. The increasing rate of cost of information sources is decreasing the number of information resources. This phenomenon leads to the development of the library consortium. There are many other reasons that led to the development of consortia in libraries, include shrinking library budget, availability of information in different forms, ever changing nature of information, availability of technology, to coordinate with other institutions, avoid the related legal issues, and many others. Some of the consortiums are.

- **INDEST Consortium** by MHRD, GOI, covering all IIT, NIT, IIM, IIIT, and other AICTE institutions.
- **CSIR Consortium:** maintained by NISCAIR, providing its services to laboratories and R&D workers of CSIR community.
- **UGC Infonet Consortium:** maintained by INFLIBNET providing services to universities and colleges in India.
- **CeRA:** Consortium for e-resources in Agriculture.
- **FORSA Consortium**
- **MCIT Consortium, etc.**

SOCIAL MEDIA

These days' social media are being used by many libraries to stay connected with users. Moreover, social media are becoming an alternative channel for communicating its users. Social media are being utilised for resources sharing if the library has digital resources. Social media are very helpful in order to reach out even least users of the library. In social media environment no need to serve for individual users but as a whole community at a single post. This is how social media play an important role in sharing information. The second law of Ranganathan 'every reader his/her book' says if, users are not coming to the library, library has to go to the users. In this regard, social media will act as a channel between library and users.

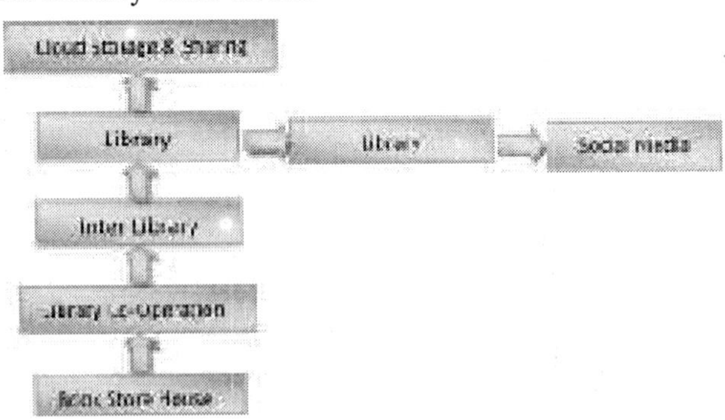

Fig. 1. Morphology of Resource Sharing and Networking in Libraries

CLOUD STORAGE SHARING

The advancement of information communication technology made a vital impact on storage technology; as a result, cloud storage technology is being used in recent past. Cloud storage technique solved the space problem in libraries. Here, only thing is that libraries should have digital resources. These resources can be stored in the cloud, later users can access these cloud stored data from any corner of the world with his/her login credentials. Some of cloud-storage applications include

- Dropbox
- Smugmug
- Synaptop
- SkyDrive from Microsoft
- GoogleDrive from Google
- Digital Locker in Digital India project are the examples of cloud storage technology, this technology made easy for resource sharing in the library community.

POPULAR SOCIAL MEDIA

Some the most popular are discussed here can be used for providing information services to the users. Some of the media offers different services so that libraries can be used different media for different services and application in order to provide effective services.

Table 1. List of popular social media, based on number of monthly users.

Sl. No.	*Name of Social Media*	*Monthly Users (As on Sept. 18, 2016)*
1	Facebook	1,710,000,000
2	YouTube	1,000,000,000
3	Instagram	500,000,000
4	Twitter	313,000,000
5	Reddit	234,000,000
6	Vine	200,000,000

7	Ask.fm	160,000,000
8	Tumblr	115,000,000
9	Flickr	112,000,000
10	Google+	111,000,000
11	LinkedIn	106,000,000
12	Pinterest	100,000,000
13	VK	90,000,000
14	ClassMates	57,000,000
15	Meetup	27,500,000

Source: www.dreamgrow.com (Top 15 popular social networking sites)

Facebook

At present time, Facebook is a dominated social networking site in terms of usage by online users. Facebook is owned by Facebook Inc. and established in 2004. It provides many applications to the users some of them include Events, Marketplace, Notes, Places, Platform, Facebook Questions, Photos, Videos, Facebook Paper, Facebook Mentions etc. sharing information, video and images through facebook is very easy.

Blogs

Blogs are more popular media among library community in order to disseminate the information to the users. There are many blogging sites allow you to develop your own library blog freely. If the finance is viable then you can create a paid blog to share your resources and services to your user community. 'Research Blogging' is an example of sharing research abstract as well as news related to it appeared on other sites. You can write and use the blog for providing services and resources; you can post digital resources for users' usage. There is also the possibility to work co-operatively with other libraries with a similar area of interest. BlogSpot, Blogger and Wordpress are allowing you to create your own blog freely.

Micro-blogging

Micro-blogging sites like Twitter, Instagram allow you to update your status. The twitter allows you to enter the 140 characters. These micro-blogging are more popular way to remain networked and share opinions about library related activities, including their services, new arrivals, events in the library, etc. even it becomes a platform for the discussion to improve your working style. Library can receive users' comments feedback; suggestion etc. for further improvement, you may use hashtag to gather the comments from the user at one place.

YouTube

It is a video sharing website among internet users. It is created in 2005 and now owned by Google since 2006. It is started its' services in India in 2008. YouTube software application can radically change the ways libraries providing services. Providing and explaining the services through video will be more effective to understand for users. Library instruction, library tour, and training can disseminate very effectively. Recorded lecture can be uploading directly to youtube and provide the links on library site. Likewise users can directly access the online lecturers.

Linked In

Linked In is a social networking site and online platform for professionals. It helps for the library professionals came under a single umbrella. It help to share the information among professionals working in different libraries in different places rather than library clientele. It provides eLearning resources, skill building job training for the professionals. It also supports for the community to digital literacy start-ups and jobs searching facilities.

Flickr

Flickr is an image sharing application media. It is the best photo management and sharing application in the online world. Its main aim is to help the public make their images available to the friends really who concerns to them and also to facilitate new organisation ways of videos and photos. For the libraries and librarians, it helps to catalogue their pictures and images to careful archiving. It is more helpful if our libraries became digital and automated.

USAGE OF SOCIAL MEDIA IN CENTRAL UNIVERSITIES

The central universities are selected for the collection of data on social media usage for students' engagements. Facebook, Twitter, LinkedIn, YouTube, google+, Blogs, Flickr, RSS/Atom are selected for the study. Total of forty six central universities five universities has the independent library website. The detail data depicted in the below table.

Table 2. Usage of Social media

Sl. No	*Name of Social Media*	*No. of Central Universities Using*	*No. of Central Universities Not Using*	*Data Not Available*	*Total*
1	Library site	5	40	1	46
2	Facebook	25	20	1	46
3	Twitter	19	26	1	46
4	LinkedIn	6	39	1	46
5	G+	14	31	1	46
6	Blogs	5	40	1	46
7	You Tube	14	31	1	46
8	RSS/Atom	5	40	1	46

Forty six central universities are established till date in India. There are 40 universities including an Open University (IGNOU) providing general education including arts, humanities, social science, science and other faculties. However, there are 6 universities specialised (Agriculture, Aviation, English, Hindi, Maritime and Urdu each one) education and research facility. Delhi and Uttar Pradesh consist of five central universities each, Bihar 3, Assam 2, Jammu and Kashmir 2, Madhya Pradesh 2, Manipur 2, Tamil

Nadu 2 and Telangana 2, and remaining states have each one excluding Goa and Andhra Pradesh.

From the above table, it is clear that most of the universities are not using the social media for students' engagement. However, it also clears more than half of universities using the Facebook (25). The remaining twitter 19, YouTube and G+ 14 each, LinkedIn 6, Blogs and RSS 5 each, used social media in central universities. In order to provide effective services through social media, libraries should construct their own website and adopt the social media.

APPLICATIONS OF SOCIAL MEDIA IN LIBRARIES

Library Marketing

Marketing the resource and services to the users is an important aspect in the library. Many libraries are actively anticipating in proving new services, repackaged and consolidated information. However, they are not marketing effectively their services and resources. If you are not advertising well your product will be not used by more customers, So that, libraries should market their services and resources. Social media are a great help in this regard, social media allow you to stay connected with users; if any product received and services launched you can share those with your users, through that they can make use of these resources and services very effectively. Libraries have to find new ways to reach out the users like business companies.

User Engagement

Social media help you to stay connect with your users and it also enables you to interact with your users. Two way communication is possible through social media. Whenever, libraries are sharing information, and then they can get feedback, comments, suggestions and appreciation regarding their services instantly, this how libraries can continuously engage with users.

Information Services

Most commonly social media are used to provide information services to the clientele. Twitter, Facebook, blogs are leading social media used for the purposes.

Collection Development and Management

What resources are needed for users is the most important element of collection development policy in the library. Social media helps libraries to take suggestions and the user wants. This will help to build a sound collection and well developed libraries.

Resource Sharing

How do users know what resources library has in its collection? If the library has electronic information, that can be shared easily with users and another library. Sharing the list of resources to the users is a greater help. This way users came to know, what resources are available in the library and then they can use it whenever they need it.

Collection Usage and Discovery

Social media will help to create awareness among users to make the best use of core journals and database. Library can share information regarding using and discovering core databases through social media. Why because libraries paid lots of money for databases and online journals to fulfil the user need.

Teaching and Learning Tool

Social media is a not only for leisure activity, it is also used for teaching and learning; teachers can share their topical ideologies through social media to the students. Students are also active and interested learning from social media as they spend lots of time on social media.

Outreach Activity

Libraries can use actively the social media for outreaching. They can use social media for promoting faculty work, library services and connection broader library user community. Faculty published work can be promote through social media. Social media can be used for creating awareness about library activities and usage and resources.

CONCLUSION

The emergence of Internet has revolutionized the library progress. Use of software for library activities, digital libraries library networking and consortium all became possible. Library must adapt to the changing face, or they will fall behind to provide efficient services to the users. Library should always conduct user studies to understanding resources and channel they prefer, the channel they prefer for use of the resource. Many of the studies proved providing information via social media is also effective. It is a tendency now among young adults usage of social media. It is better to adopt the social media technology in order to provide efficient services to its patrons.

REFERENCES

1. Anjali Singh (2016). Delhi traffic police: social media for better traffic management, Emerald Emerging Markets Case Studies,
2. Carl Gustav Johannsen, (2015). Teaching social media in public libraries – Danish experiences, The Bottom Line, Vol. 28 Iss 1/2 pp. 19 – 25
3. CILIP (2016). Five ways libraries are using social media access on 29/09/2016; available at: http://www.cilip.org.uk/blog/5wayslibrariesareusingsocialmedia
4. du Toit, Karen & Mulatiningsih, Bekti (2013). Social media for libraries. In Information & Library Management Africa, 26 Sept. 2013, Johannesburg, South Africa
5. Fernandez, Joe (2009). A SWOT Analysis for Social Media in Libraries, Library Staff Publications. P. 07, http://digitalcommons.library.umaine.edu/lib_staffpub/7
6. Flickr.com, available at https://www.flickr.com/about/ accessed on 29/9/2016
7. Gadad, Ruju and Gurikar, Rushmanasab (2015) Libraries Services, Users Requirements and Social Media: Building Relationships via Social Networks, National Conference on

Library Information Science & Information Technology for Education, ISBN: 1-63102-455-8, 27-August, 2015, Modern Rohini Education Society; Web Conference http://rtmonline.in/proceeding/ncite15-proceeding.pdf

8. Hadewijch Vanwynsberghe Elke Boudry Ruben Vanderlinde Pieter Verdegem (2014). Experts as facilitators for the implementation of social media in the library? A social network approach, Library Hi Tech, Vol. 32 Iss 3 pp. 529 – 545

9. Jotham Wasike, (2013). Social media ethical issues: role of a librarian, Library Hi Tech News, Vol. 30 Iss 1 pp. 8 – 16

10. Joyce Garczynski , (2016). #Donate: the role of social media in academic library fundraising, The Bottom Line, Vol. 29 Iss 2 pp. 60 – 66

11. Khan, Shakeel Ahmad, & Bhatti, Rubina (2012). Application of social media in marketing of library and information services: A case study from Pakistan. Webology, 9(1)

12. Luo Lili Wang Yuan Han Lifeng , (2013). Marketing via social media: a case study, Library Hi Tech, Vol. 31 Iss 3 pp. 455 -466

13. McCreadie, N (2013). Library Value in the Developing World. IFLA Journal 39(3): 327-343.

14. Michael Ahenkorah-Marfo Harry Akussah , (2016). Changing the face of reference and user services, Reference Services Review, Vol. 44 Iss 3 pp. 219 – 236

15. Popular SNS available at http://www.dreamgrow.com/top-15-most-popular-social-networking-sites/ accessed on 18/9/2016

16. Sanjeev Prashar , Nishanth Shri Kara and Harvinder Singh (2013). Mumbai Indians: a case on social media marketing, Emerald Emerging Markets Case Studies,

17. Suraya Hamid Sarah Bukhari Sri Devi Ravana Azah Anir Norman Mohamad Taha Ijab , (2016). Role of social media in information-seeking behaviour of international students, Aslib Journal of Information Management, Vol. 68 Iss 5 pp. 643 – 666

18. UGC: central universities: available at www.ugc.ac.in/centraluniversity.aspx

5

Digital Libraries and Its Future

Milind Mohan Dubal
Librarian
Institute of Management & Computer Studies, Thane, Maharashtra

ABSTRACT

Information technology plays a vital role in the field of library and information technology. Libraries are now becoming computerized and digitized. Digital library is the need for future generation. Many rare and old works, documents etc. are needed to be digitized, so that future generation can take advantage of it as well as these materials can be preserved forever. This paper is focusing especially on digital libraries and its usefulness and why these digital libraries are beneficial for the future generation.

Keywords : Library, Digital Library, Traditional Libraries, Features of Digital Library, Benefits of Digital Library.

INTRODUCTION

A Digital Library is a library in which collections are stored in digital formats such as print format, microform format and other media and accessible through computers. The digital content may be stored locally, or accessed remotely via computer networks. A digital library is a type of information retrieval system. Depending on the specific library, a user may be able to access magazine articles, books, papers, images, sound files and video.

Digital libraries are organizations that provide the resources, including the specialized staff, to select, structure, offer intellectual access to interpret, distribute, preserve the integrity of, and ensure the persistence over time of collections of digital works so that they are readily and economically available for use by a community or set of communities.

According to Terence R. Smith "Controlled collections of information bearing objects that are in digital from those may be organized accessed, evaluated and used by means of a heterogeneous and extensive set of distributed services that are supported by digital technology".

FEATURES DIGITAL LIBRARIES

Collection of digitized documents, image and sounds can be accessed and read by the users on computers,

- Easy retrieval of information.
- Multi-platform: User can access from anywhere without the physical presence of resources.
- Preservation and conservation: All the materials which are old and are repeatedly used can be preserved and conserved for future use.
- Available 24/7: it is open all the days of the year, although 24 hours.
- It reduces space problem in the large Libraries.
- Institutional repository: It helps in the creation of institutional repository by adding intuitions books, papers, thesis, dissertation and other works.

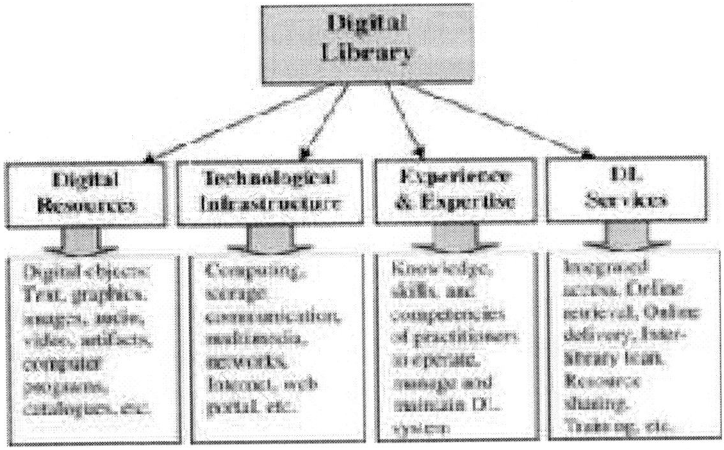

BENEFITS OF DIGITAL LIBRARIES

Digital libraries bring significant benefits to the users through the following features:

Improved access

Digital libraries are typically accessed through the Internet and Compact Disc-Read Only Memory (CD-ROM). They can be accessed virtually from anywhere and at any time. They are not tied to the physical location and operating hours of at traditional library.

Wider access

A digital library can meet simultaneous access requests for a document by easily creating multiple instances or copies of the requested document. It can also meet the requirements of a larger population of users easily.

Improved information sharing

Through the appropriate metadata and information exchange protocols, the digital libraries can easily share information with other similar digital libraries and provide enhanced access to users.

Improved preservation

Since the electronic documents are not prone to physical wear and tear, their exact copies can easily be made, the digital libraries facilitate preservation of special and rare documents and artefacts by providing access to digital versions of these entities.

FUNCTIONAL COMPONENTS OF DIGITAL LIBRARY

Most digital libraries share common functional components. These include:

Selection and acquisition

The typical processes covered in this component include the selection of documents to be added, the subscription of the database and the digitization or conversion of documents to an appropriate digital form.

Organization

The key process involved in this component is the assignment of the metadata to each document being added to the collection.

Indexing and storage : This component carries out the indexing and storage of documents and metadata for efficient search and retrieval.

Search and retrieval

This is the digital library interface used by the end users to browse, search, retrieve and view the contents of the digital library. These mentioned components are the important characteristic of the digital library, which differ it from others collections of online information.

FUTURE OF DIGITAL LIBRARIES

Large scale digitization projects are underway at Google, the Million Book Project and Internet Archive. With continued improvements in book handling and presentation technologies such as optical character recognition and eBooks, development of alternative depositories and business models, digital libraries are rapidly growing in popularity as demonstrated by Google, Yahoo and MSN,s efforts. Just as libraries have ventured into audio and video collections, so have digital libraries such as the Internet Archive.

WHAT FUTURE DO WE SEE?

- Structured access
- Browse and search features appropriate to the content
- Importance of metadata, as approach to the digital document
- Distributed digital collections transparent access
- Submission support, alerting services

Lynch (1994) says that "digital Libraries... [provide] users with coherent success to a very large, organized repository of information and knowledge." According to Berkeley Digital Library Project, University of California, the digital library will be a collection of distributed information sources. The contrast between traditional and digital libraries is presented below.

Sl. No.	*Traditional Libraries*	*Digital or Electronic Library*
1.	Print collection	All resources in digital form.
2.	Stable, with slow evolution	Dynamic and ephemeral
3.	Individual objects not directly linked with each other.	Multi-media and fractal objects
4.	Flat structure with minimal contextual metadata	The scaffolding of data structures and richer contextual metadata.
5.	Scholarly content with validation process	More than scholarly content with various validation processes
6.	Limited access points and centralized management	Unlimited access points, distributed collections and access control

7.	The physical and logical organization correlated.	The physical and logical organization may be virtually
8.	One way interactions	Dynamic real-time dialogue
9.	Free and universal access.	Free as well as fee based.

CONCLUSION

Librarians need to improve new skills while using librarianship and information profession. Librarians must achieve the new skills such as networking, web-based technologies, and Cloud based service, online searching of electronic database, e-journals etc. Digital library is simply the most current and most widely accepted term and is now used almost exclusively in online searches and in the literature. Digital libraries are getting very useful for ready access and future preservation of rare, old and some fragile documents. Digitization has changed the atmosphere of libraries from converting them traditional to digital libraries.

REFERENCES

1. http://www.webpages.uidaho.edu/~mbolin/trivedi-diglib.htm
2. https://www.google.co.in/search?q=digital+library&client=firefox-b-ab&source=lnms&tbm=isch& sa=X&ved= 0ahUKEwj7wauploTPAhXIsY8KHR6ZBdMQ _AUICCgB&biw=1024&bih=657#imgrc=5z9yNH2rTlqn-M%3A
3. https://www.google.co.in/search?q=digital+library&client=firefox-b-ab&source =lnms &tbm =isch &sa= X&ved =0ahUKEwj7wauploTPAhXIsY8KHR6ZBdMQ _AUICCgB&biw=1024&bih=657#imgrc=5z9yNH2rTlqn-M%3A
4. Singh, S.A.; Barse, N.S.; Savanur, S.K.; Joshi, P.P. (2011). Post-Modernisation of Librarianship. Thane : K.G. Joshi Bedekar College.
5. Fadake, D. (2008). Granthalya Saganikaran Avn Adhunikaran. New Delhi : Universal Prakashan.

6

Redefining Digital Library in the Light of Modern Context

Navneet Kumar Sharma
Junior Research Fellow
Department of Library and Information Science
Banaras Hindu University, Varanasi, U.P.

ABSTRACT

This paper is to examine the definition of a digital library. It is important to get an exact understanding about a typical digital library Digital library is not only "library without walls" or "library without books" but it is something beyond these traditional stereotypic definitions. It is important to define the term properly as to be distinguished from other technical terms like electronic or virtual library. A definition is a statement of the meaning of a term (a word, phrase, or another set of symbols. The definition should be something that can make the particular term more clear and distinct. A good definition explains what something means in very concise manner. The definition should be ideally complete and perfect in explaining all the attributes of the term. The definition should be flawless in explaining its meaning. The methodology opted for this study is definitions extracted from various articles published in national and international journals; and also from internet sources like Wikipedia. Digital libraries appear different things to different people. As far as library and information science is concerned, we should have to move forward in an evolutionary way instead of a revolutionary way. Digital library provides a coherent view of all of the information presents within a library, without considering its form or format. There is need of a working definition of a digital library because it will add more clarity to library and information science field and to the knowledge of common man.

Keywords : Digital library, definition, library.

INTRODUCTION

According to Dr. S. R. Ranganathan, "A library is a trinity of user, staff and documents". In the context of digital library, the format of "documents" is changed. Traditional documents are now famed as digital objects that include different file formats such as text, images, pdf, audio, visual etc. (born digital or converted digital). There are hundreds of digital libraries installed in the world. Correspondingly, there are hundreds of definitions of a digital library. The Information Infrastructure Technology and Application (IITA) Working Group consider 'digital libraries as systems providing users with coherent access to a very large, organized repository of information and knowledge.' Larson defined digital libraries as "no single, stand-alone, repositories of digital data. Instead, they are a heterogeneous collection of network-based repositories using a variety of protocols of users (and repositories) interaction, data encoding and transmission." According to 'Association of Research Libraries', "a digital library is not a single entity, requires technology to link the resources of many, linkage transparent to the users, permits universal access, not limited to document surrogates but extended to digital artefacts." Noerr suggested two possibilities for a digital library, either a 'library that contains material in the digitized form'; or a 'library that contains digital material.

There are other definitions like 'library without walls' or 'library without books' and synonymous terms such as electronic library or virtual library. Digital libraries may be treated as of high-quality information contained in digital form on diverse format permitting access over different electronic networks. Digital libraries aim at unhindered access to contents over computer and communication networks. Digital libraries are the backbone of a country or state who wants to be called as developed one. A library in any form either traditional or digital is always useful for the society. So what can be a working definition for a digital library? In this paper I, tried my genuine efforts to make the term "digital libraries" more transparent from its definition point of view.

WHAT IS A DEFINITION?

A definition is a statement of the meaning of a term (a word, phrase, or another set of symbols). It lists every single object described by the term. A term may have multiples meanings, contexts and different senses, that is why a term is require multiple definitions. Therefore every term has many definitions. The definition should be something that can make the particular term more clear and distinct. A good definition explains what something means in very concise manner. The definition should be ideally complete and perfect in explaining all the attributes of the term. The definition should be flawless in explaining its meaning. The definition is clearness or sharpness of an image or an object. It can be related to the degree of distinctness.

DEFINING DIGITAL LIBRARY

One of the important factors in defining digital library is the definition is dependent on the community of people who are using it. Digital library is the focal point of varied areas as stated by Nurnberg et al, 1995. It has been described differently in different areas. Few examples are stated in following lines.

- It is a large database from an information retrieval system (IRS) point of view.
- It is a particular application based on hypertext methods for people working on hypertext technology.

- It is an application of web for people who are working on wide-area information delivery.
- And for library and information science, it is nothing but another step in continuing automation of libraries.

These above definitions actually add more developments to the digital library. Digital libraries can be defined in many ways. Some of the prominent definitions scattered in various articles is mentioned below:-

- The digital library is the collection of services and the collection of information objects that support users in dealing with information objects available directly or indirectly via electronic/digital means. (Leiner,1998)
- A managed collection of information, with associated services, where the information is stored in digital formats and accessible over a network (Arms, 2000).
- Digital libraries are organizations that provide the resources, including the specialized staff, to select, structure, offer intellectual access to, interpret, distribute, preserve the integrity of, and ensure the persistence over time of collections of digital works so that they are readily and economically available for use by a defined community or set of communities (The Digital Library Federation's 2003).
- Resources are available in a machine-readable format (as opposed to print or microform), accessible by means of computers (Kresh, 2007).
- Numerous medium resource groups of distribution, super large-scale and easy conversion and thus people can get information services which cannot be restricted by time or regions via the internet (Li, 2002).
- Digital libraries are organizations that provide the resources, including the specialized staff, to select, structure, offer intellectual access to, interpret, distribute, preserve the integrity of, and ensure the persistence over time of collections of digital works so that they are readily and economically available for

use by a defined community or set of communities (Waters, 1988).

SOME MORE DEFINITIONS

The term digital refers to something using digits, particularly binary digits (Wikipedia). "A digital library is a special library with a focused collection of digital objects that can include text, visual material, audio material, video material, stored as electronic media formats (as opposed to print, microform, or other media), along with means for organizing, storing, and retrieving the files and media contained in the library collection. Digital libraries can vary immensely in size and scope and can be maintained by individuals, organizations, or affiliated with established physical library buildings or institutions, or with academic institutions. The electronic content may be stored locally, or accessed remotely via computer networks. An electronic library is a type of information retrieval system" (Wikipedia). A digital library is characterized by digital documents in a digital environment. Serves a defined community or set of communities; may not be a single entity; are underpinned by a unified and logical organizational structure; incorporate learning as well as access; make the most of human ("librarian") as well as technological resources; provide fast and efficient accessing, with multiple access modes; provide free access to a community or communities; own and control their resources; have collections that are large and persist over time, are well organized and managed, contain many formats, contain objects, not just representations, contain objects that are unobtainable, and contain some objects that are solely digital (Schwartz, 2000).

COMPONENTS OF DIGITAL LIBRARY

Components required for a digital library can broadly be categorized into the following components (Arora, 2008)

- Collection Infrastructure
- Digital Resource Organization

- Access Infrastructure
- Computer and Network Infrastructure
- IPR and Digital Rights Management
- Digital Library Services

PURPOSE OF DIGITAL LIBRARY

- Collect, store and organize knowledge in digital form.
- Promote economic and efficient delivery of information.
- Leverage the considerable investments in computing/ communications infrastructure.
- Strengthen communication and collaboration between research, business, government and educational communities.
- Contribute to lifelong learning opportunities.

FUNCTIONS OF DIGITAL LIBRARY

- Identification and collection of contents to be digitized.
- Classification and digitization of these contents.
- Editing, formatting and storage of the contents
- Designing search engines to selectively search and access the contents.
- Publishing contents digitally for end-user access.
- Transforming printed information into digital form.
- Storage, retrieval and handling of easy-to-use, electronic information.
- Converting data from diverse media or formats into different formats. Classification techniques for improving retrieval efficiency.
- Managing devices for large massive storage, with multilevel hierarchical storage structures, supporting differing speed storage devices and varied capacity processors.

- Editing and formatting of contents in HTML, VRML, PDF, JPEG, etc.
- Browsing and querying facilities for content-based retrieval.

CONCLUSION

Digital library is indeed a necessity in present knowledge-based society. Therefore a proper and valid definition is the demand of today. The definitions provided in this paper are much more relevant to define digital libraries in the appropriate context. The users will find these definitions very precise and accurate as far as modern day context digital library is concerned. The definition given by Ranganthan is undoubtedly, the best description of a library which can be equally applicable on digital library, unaltered. Therefore, the digital library is far more than "library without walls" or "library without books". Digital library surpasses greater dimensions across the world. In simple words, digital libraries are the digital face of traditional libraries.

REFERENCES

1. Arms, W.Y. (2000), Digital Libraries, MIT Press, Cambridge, MA.
2. Arora, J. (2001) Indian National Digital Library in Engineering Science and Technology (INDEST): A proposal for strategic co-operation for consortia-based access to electronic resources. The International Information & Library Review 33 (2-3), 149-165
3. Association of Research Libraries (1995). Definition and Purposes of a Digital Library, October 23, 1995.Retrieved fromhttp://sunsite.berkeley.edu/ARL/definition.html
4. Cleveland, Gary (1998.. Digital Libraries: Definitions, issues and challenges. IFLA, Universal dataflow and telecommunications core programme, March, 1998.
5. Definition - Wikipedia, the free encyclopedia.Retrieved fromhttps://en.wikipedia.org/wiki/Difinition
6. Digital - Wikipedia, the free encyclopedia.Retrieved fromhttps://en.wikipedia.org/wiki/Digital
7. Digital Library Initiatives. Building Digital Libraries: Digital Library Projects. The University of Texas at Austin Library Online,

June 7, 2001.Retrieved fromhttp://www.lib.utexas.edu/dli/digital.html

8. Digital Library - Wikipedia, the free encyclopedia.Retrieved fromhttps://en.wikipedia.org/wiki/Digital_library
9. Kresh, D. (2007), The Whole Digital Library Handbook, American Library Association, Chicago, IL.
10. Larson, Ray R. Search Capabilities for Users of Digital Libraries: Tools and Paradigms. Retrieved fromhttp://is.gseis.ucla.edu/research/dl/larson.html
11. Leiner, B.M. (1998), "The NCSTRL approach to open architecture for the confederated digital library", D-Lib Magazine. Retrieved fromwww.dlib.org/dlib/december98/leiner/12leiner.html
12. Li, G. (2002). Digital Libraries Research, Peking Library Publishing House, Peking. Retrieved from http://www-diglib.stanford.edu/diglib/pub/reports/iita-dlw/
13. Lynch, Clifford and Garcia-Molina, Hector (1995). Interoperability, Scaling, and the Digital Libraries Research Agenda: A Report on the May 18-19, 1995, IITA Digital Libraries Workshop, August 22, 1995. Retrieved fromhttp://www.itrd.gov/pubs/iita-dlw/main.html
14. Noerr, Peter. The Digital Library Toolkit, March 2000.Retrieved fromhttp://www.sun.com.products-n-solutions/edu/libraries/digitaltoolkit.html
15. Nurnberg, P.J., Furuta, R., Leggett, J.J., Marshall, C., and Shipman III, F.M. (1995). Digital libraries: issues and architectures. In Proceedings of the Second Annual Conference on the Theory and Practice of Digital Libraries. Austin, Texas, June 11-13, 1995, pp. 147-153.
16. Ranganathan, S. R. (1931), The Five Laws of Library Science. Asia Publishing House, Bombay, 1931.
17. Schwartz, C. (2000). Digital libraries: an overview, The Journal of Academic Librarianship, Vol. 26 No. 6, pp. 385-93.
18. Waters, D.J. (1998). What are digital libraries? CLIR Issues,July/August. Retrieved from http://www.clir.org/pubs/issues/issues04.HTML

7

Institutional Repository and Their Role

Abhilasha Priyadarshani
Research Scholar
Dept. of Library & Information science
Banaras Hindu University, Varanasi- 221005, U.P.

ABSTRACT

This chapter aims to explain an overview of Institutional repositories (IR). This may help to know the brief idea about IR, and related issues regarding the history of IR in India, open access IR, software, characteristics, need and role of IR. IR is an online platform that ensures the access, preservation and dissemination of scholarly output of parent institute. It is maintained by parent institution itself. An institutional repository is defined as "a service that enables the organization preservation and dissemination of the scholarly output of an institute. Repository items are born digital or digitized, tagged with metadata to describe the subject, ownership, copyright and structure; indexed; organized into collections and searchable via the web; and preserved for long-term access. There are different kinds of software available for developing IR. DSpace, Eprint and Fedora are some widely used software for developing IR. It has potential to play an important role in the current scholarly communication system. For enhancing teaching learning and research through dissemination of scholarly output of the Institution.

Keywords:

INTRODUCTION

ICT has impacted on every sphere of academic library activity especially in the form of the library collection development strategies, library building and consortia. ICT presents an opportunity to provide value-added information services and access to a wide variety of digital based information resources to their clients. (Krubu Kingsley Efe Osawaru, 2011). Impact of ICT on LIS means the application of computers and communication technology to the acquisition, organization, storage, retrieval and dissemination of information process. Convergence of computer and communication technologies and their subsequent application to library and information activities has changed the philosophy of information from unitary to universal access (Santha Devi Antherjanam & N K Sheeja, 2008). There are lots of changes taken place in libraries such as e-resources, automation, open educational resources, digital curation, open resource movement, information literacy, open archiving, etc. and the Institutional repository is one of them. All these changes are made to facilitate better services to users and the meantime these changes are forcing the library professional to improve their skills. In this chapter we will learn:

- What is Institutional Repository?
- The content of an IR.
- Need of IR
- Role of IR in scholarly communication, etc.

WHAT IS AN INSTITUTIONAL REPOSITORY?

An institutional repository or IR is an online platform that allows access to and preserves work created and deposited by members of that scholarly community (Geoffrey Little, 2011). The national institute of health library defines an institutional repository as "a service that enables the organization preservation and dissemination of the scholarly output of an institute.... Repository items are born digital or digitized, tagged with metadata to describe the subject, ownership, copyright and structure; indexed; organized into collections and searchable via the web; and preserved for long-term access. Institutional repositories are "digital collection that captures and preserves the intellectual output of a single or multi-university community" (crow, 2002).

Lynch defines institutional repository as "a set of services that a university offers to the members of its community for the management and dissemination of digital material created by the institution and its community members. It is most essentially an organizational commitment to a stewardship, of these digital materials including long-term preservation where appropriate as well as the organization and access or distribution". (Lynch, 2003). Institutional repositories are not serving as an information provider to its parent institutions and their patrons but also giving a chance to the faculty members and researchers to contribute themselves with information depositing. A simple definition of IR is web based-archive (Johnson, 2007) or digital collection (Crow, 2002) of scholarly materials produced by members of the parent institution. Different authors define institutional repository in different words.

Institutional repositories (IR) are defined by Piorun et al. (2007) as electronic systems that capture, preserve, and provide access to the intellectual output of a community in a digital format. The goal of an IR is to collect, preserve, and make persistently accessible a variety of scholarly materials (Palmer et al., 2008). Open access digital repositories have implemented the Open Archive Initiative Protocol for Metadata Harvesting (OAI-PMH) as a mechanism to achieve interoperability in the exchange of meta-information with other systems (Muhammad et al, 2007). With all the different software platforms employed by IRs, their systems need to be able to support interoperability in order to provide access via multiple online search engines (Tmava, A. M., & Alemneh, D. G, 2013)

According to Heery & Anderson (2005) Institutional Repositories:

Contains content, deposited by owner, creator, or third party;

- Repository architecture manages content as well as metadata;
- Repository offers a minimum set of basic services, e.g. put, get, search, access control;
- Repository must be sustainable and trusted, well-supported and well managed;
- If an Open Access Repository, it must also:
- Provide Open access to its content (notwithstanding legal constraints);
- Provide Open access to its metadata for harvesting.

Simply we can understand that an institutional repository is a platform created by an institute, where all the scholars, faculty members and others (define by the policy) of that institute can share (store, preserve) their research outcome.

OPEN ACCESS IR

"Open access is free online access to peer-reviewed research" (http://users.ecs.soton.ac.uk/harnad/Temp/liege22.mov); this is how Stevan Harnad defines open access in his address to the European Rectors' meeting on open access which took place at the University of Liege on October 18, 2007. Institutional repositories (IRs), one of the media for providing open access (Cantavaridou, 2008).

In the recent years, the proponents of open access to scholarly information are strongly urging the institutions to set up interoperable, open-access institutional repositories and impress upon their researchers to self-archive a copy of their research publications in such repositories. Institutional repositories will give better visibility to the research papers that they hold because any person with access to the Internet will be able to read and download research papers contained in open-access repositories. After all, any researcher would want their research work to be read and be cited by as many people as possible. There is no better way of realizing this than through the open-access repositories. Studies have shown that research articles that are available in open-access repositories get better citations than the ones that are subscription-based (Lawrence, 2001).

In 2007, the working group of the National Knowledge Commission (NKC) on 'Open Access and Open Educational Resources' recommended in their report to increase Open Access content from India, in order to increase the public awareness and utilization of OA material. During 2004 to 2008 approximately 12 repositories were developed in India and the majority of the repositories revolved around scientific and research organizations (Sawant, 2011).

"Institutional repositories are inherently tied to open access movement." (Ronald C.J. and Wilson M.C, 2008). Mostly institutional repositories are having collections of research publications, thesis, dissertations, annual reports and institutional publications. Earlier the institutional repositories are restricted accessibility of their collections to the staff, researchers and users of the parent organization but the scenario is changing gradually. "All of the repositories permit free access to abstracts without any registration necessary. However, most of the repositories require the user to register for accessing the full text of items." (Tripathi M. and Jeevan V.K.J., 2011) Typically speaking, about India, as an approximation government funds for 75% of education and 95% of research. The results of research funded by government should ideally be accessible in open access to the society at large because the major source of government funds is from its citizens. Funding agencies like National Institute of Health in the United States & Welcome Trust in the UK have already mandated submission of results of research funded by them in open access journals or make them available in open access. Moreover, Articles in open access have greater impact in terms of citation rates than those published in subscription-based journals; Open access means easier access to knowledge, so more researchers can build on that knowledge without duplication of efforts, reaching larger audience with greater access and more citations, Institutions are also benefited as their research becomes more visible adding to the reputation of the institute (Yatrik Patel).

CHARACTERISTICS OF IR

The scholarly publishing and academic resources coalition (SPARC) position paper Crow identifies four essential characteristics of IR:

- institutionally defined;
- scholarly;
- cumulative and perpetual;
- open and interoperable"

SOFTWARE FOR IR

There are numbers of software for content management and developing Institutional repository. Some of them are open sources and some of them are proprietary software.

Open source software

Open source software is computer software which is available for all free of cost or it may charge a nominal cost (for some of its extended services). Open source software available with its source code so that user can use, share and change according to their requirement. Examples: DSpace, Eprint, Fedora, Greenstone, etc.

Proprietary software

In contrary to open source software, proprietary software is made for monitory gain. Users have to take permission or a license to use this kind of software. We can use this software and to some extent. We can customize it but we can not make a change in it because its source code is not open for its users. Example: Digital commons and Simple DL etc.

DSPACE

Dspace developed by MIT Libraries in collaboration with Hewlett-Packard, to establish an institutional repository for MIT has been released in November 2002 in Cambridge, Massachusetts. Most recently version 1.4 was released in July 2006. DSpace is an open source software package which provides the tools for management of digital assets and is commonly used as the basis for an institutional repository. It is also intended as a platform for Digital preservation activities. Since its release in 2002, as a product of the HP-MIT Alliance, it has been installed and is in production at over 100 institutions around the globe from large universities to small higher education colleges and research centres (http://en.wikipedia.org/wiki/DSpace).

EPRINTS

E print is free, open source software for generating an "Open Access" (OA) "Institutional Repository" (IR) that is compliant with the "Open Archives Initiative Protocol for Metadata Harvesting"(OAI-PMH) Eprints was created in 2000 as a direct outcome of the 1999 Santa Fe meeting that launched what eventually became the OAI-PMH. The Eprints software was enthusiastically received, became the first and still, the most widely used free OA IR software, and has since inspired many emulations. (http://en.wikipedia.org/wiki/Eprints).

FEDORA

Fedora (or Flexible Extensible Digital Object Repository Architecture) Fedora is developed jointly by Cornell University Information Science and the University of Virginia Library. The Fedora Project is currently supported by generous grants from the Andrew W. Mellon Foundation. Fedora is a digital asset management (DAM) architecture, upon which many types of digital library systems might be built. For an institution seeking a powerful, 636 well-architected repository suitable for very large (1,00,000) plus collections, and that have the technical expertise to support it, Fedora is a possible solution. (http://en.wikipedia.org/wiki/Fedora_%28software%29)

IR MAY CONTAIN FOLLOWING DOCUMENTS

Preprints, Working papers, Thesis, Dissertations, Conference proceedings, Books, Journals, Maps, Audio-video, Software, Blogs, Institutions publication, Annual report, Newspaper, Course syllabi, class notes, handouts, outlines, assignments prepared by faculty, lecturers, teaching assistants, and other professional teaching personnel, Other learning objects such as simulations, models, software demonstration files, images, video prepared by faculty, lecturers, teaching assistants, and other professional teaching personnel, Class notes, outlines, assignments, papers, and projects prepared by students of that institute etc.

HISTORY OF IR IN INDIA

The repository movement in India started mainly after 2002 and described by many researchers (Ghosh & Das, 2007; Swan, 2008; Alexander & Gautam, 2006; Venkadesan, 2009; Nazima & Devib, 2008; Das, Sen & Dutta, 2005; Fernandez, 2006; Anuradha, 2005; Arunachalam, 2008; Ghosh, 2007 & 2009; Gobbur, 2007; Kataria, 2007). Bangalore declaration (2006) drafted a model National Open Access Policy for Developing Countries also support this view and advocated for the open access institutional repository.

ePrints@IISc (http://eprints.iisc.ernet.in) is India's first interoperable, open-access institutional repository to have been established. The then director of the Institute, Professor Govardhan Mehata had officially launched the ePrints@IISc service in September 2002.

NEED OF IR

India has a vast higher education system. By May 2015, India has 712 universities, 330 of which are state universities, 46 central universities, 128 deemed universities and 208 private universities; 16 IITs, 8 IIMs, 8 IIITs, 20 NITs, 4; NITRs. Every year these huge higher academic institutions are producing thousands of research outputs in the form of theses and dissertations (TDs) but most of these TDs are underutilised and laying obscure in the libraries of TDs producing institutions due to lack of suitable access system (Sarkar & Mukhopadhyay,2016). For this, we need a platform that may store, preserve and disseminate all the scholarly output so utilization of resources can be maximised. And Institutional repository is one of the best options for fulfilling this purpose.

There are so many things that insist a need or IR and one of them is a serial crisis. Because of serial crisis, the subscription of large no. of journals are seemed unaffordable for most of the libraries. Open access resources are emerging as a solution to this problem and IR facilitating open access as well.

ROLE OF IR

For preserving, managing and long-term accessibility of your works

Repository means a place where something can be store or manage. An institutional repository provides a platform to their patrons to store, preserve and manage all their scholarly works. Because of information explosion volume of literature is increasing rapidly. Every institution is facing problem to manage the same. Institutional repositories are playing a very important role to overcome this problem. If an institute creates their repository, it will help in preserving, managing and long term accessibility of their research outcome.

Role in interoperability or information sharing

According to Hirwade (2011), "interoperability is the ability of systems, services and organizations to work together and exchange information and use exchanged information without the special effort of either system" (p.59). Metadata interoperability facilitates the exchange of information between repositories and enables World Wide Web searching. To make items discoverable in the diverse online environment, the database needs to provide standards-compliant database servers and expose the fullness of that metadata to a metasearch search client (Dorman, 2008).

For betterment of institutional visibility and prestige

Foster & Gibbson (2005) found that faculty wants to be able to make their own work available to others and have easy access to other people's work. IRs also serves as tangible indicators of an institution's productivity and thereby increasing an institution's visibility, prestige and value. Beside this, it has potential to play an important role in the current scholarly communication system like:

- For transforming local publication into global publication.
- For restricting plagiarism.
- For enhancing teaching learning and research through dissemination of scholarly output of the Institutions.
- For maximizing the utilization of your work.
- For improving quality by peer review.etc.

CONCLUSION

By the end this, chapter we have a brief idea about IR, and related issues regarding the history of IR in India, open access IR, software, characteristics, need and role of IR. IR is an online platform that, ensure the access, preservation and dissemination of scholarly output of parent institute. It is maintained by parent institution itself. An institutional repository is defined as "a service that enables the organization preservation and dissemination of the scholarly output of an institute.... Repository items are born digital or digitized, tagged with metadata to describe the subject, ownership, copyright and structure; indexed; organized into collections and searchable via the web; and preserved for long-term access. There are different kinds of software available for developing IR. DSpace, Eprint and Fedora are some widely used software for developing IR. It has potential to play an important role in the current scholarly communication system. For enhancing teaching learning and research through dissemination of scholarly output of the Institutions.

REFERENCE

1. Krubu, D.E & Osawaru, K. E (2011): Impact of Information Communication Technology (ICT) on Nigerian University Libraries. http://digitalcommons.unl.edu/libphilprac/583
2. Bangalore Declaration. (2006). A National Open Access Policy for Developing Countries. http://www.ncsi.iisc.ernet.in/OAworkshop2006/pdfs/NationalOAPolicyDCs.pdf
3. Dorman, D. (2008). The potential of metasearching as an "open" service. Library Hi Tech, 26(1), 58- 67.Retrived from www.emeraldinsight.com/0737-8831.htm
4. Hirwade, M. (2011). A study of metadata standards. Library Hi Tech News, 28(7), 18-25. doi:10.1108/07419051111184052
5. Tmava, A. M., & Alemneh, D. G. (2013). Enhancing content visibility in institutional repositories: Overview of factors that affect digital resources discoverability. iConference 2013 Proceedings (pp. 855-859). doi:10.9776/13437
6. Piorun, Mary E., Comes, James F., & Billings, M. (2007). The Role of the Institutional Repository in Preserving the Scholarly Record of the University of Massachusetts". Research on Institutional Repositories: Articles and Presentations. Paper 63. Retrieved from http://digitalcommons.bepress.com/repository-research/63
7. Sarika Sawant (2011): Past and Present Scenario of Open Access Movement in India
8. Manorama Tripathi and V.K.J. Jeevan ,(2011): An Evaluation of Digital Libraries and Institutional Repositories in India

9. Crow, R. (2002). The case for institutional repositories: a SPARC position paper. Available at: www.arl.org/sparc/IR/ir.html

10. Geoffrey Little (2011): MANAGING TECHNOLOGY Solutions in Search of Problems? The Challenges and Opportunities of Institutional Repositories

11. Ronald C. Jantz and Myoung C. Wilson (2008): Institutional Repositories: Faculty Deposits, Marketing, and the Reform of Scholarly Communication

12. Yatrik Patel (2011): Institutional Repositories: A primer

13. Lynch, C. 2003. Institutional repositories: essential infrastructure for scholarship in the digital age. ARL Bimonthly Report

14. Lawrence, S. (2001), "Online or invisible?", Nature, Vol. 411 No. 6837, p. 521

15. Johnson, R.K. (2002), "Institutional repositories: partnering with faculty to enhance scholarly communication", D-Lib Magazine, Vol. 8 No. 11, available at: www.dlib.org/dlib/november02/johnson/11johnson.html

16. Alan Burk Muhammad Al-Digeil Dominic Forest Jennifer Whitney, (2007),"New possibilities for metadata creation in an institutional repository context", OCLC Systems & Services: International digital library perspectives, Vol. 23 Iss 4 pp. 403 – 410 Permanent link to this document: http://dx.doi.org/10.1108/10650750710831547

17. Elisavet Chantavaridou, (2009),"Open access and institutional repositories in Greece: progress so far", OCLC Systems & Services: International digital library perspectives, Vol. 25 Iss 1 pp. 47 – 59 Permanent link to this document: http://dx.doi.org/10.1108/10650750910931922

8

Changing Paradigm of Open Access Institutional Repositories : An Overview

Aslam Ansari
Assistant Librarian
Central Library, Integral University, Lucknow, U.P.

ABSTRACT

The IR collects and preserves the intellectual output of the institution's faculty, students, researchers and scientists in digital form, and makes it accessible to end-users. It can be made freely accessible in the form of open access institutional repositories (IRs). This paper gives an overview of open access institutional repository developed by university & research institution as reported by monitoring initiatives such as Open DOAR (Open Directory of Open Access Repositories). It also explores the number and types of documents archive, software platforms used for launching the IRs and describe the growth and development of institutional repository in world context.

Keyword : OAI, IR, Open access, open doar, OSS, Digital commons

INTRODUCTION

The institutional repository (IR) concept was born out of competition for who was going to be responsible for dissemination of an institution's intellectual product via the Internet. Scientists and Researchers generate a lot of intellectual property in various forms such as research papers, articles, books and patents etc. which can be used for the improvement of society and for further research. Thus, it becomes essential to make research accessible toot hers. Research literature can be made freely accessible in the form of open access journals, institutional repositories (IRs) or open archives, open courseware, self-posting on author's homepages and soon (Bjork, 2004). Open access to the literature, means its free availability on the public internet, permitting any users to read, download, copy, distribute, print, search or link to the full texts of these articles, crawl them for indexing, pass them as data to software, or use them for any other lawful purpose, without financial, legal, or technical barriers (Budapest Open Access Initiative, 2002).

INSTITUTIONAL REPOSITORY

An institutional repository is an online archive for collecting, preserving, and disseminating digital copies of the intellectual output of an institution, particularly a research institution. On behalf of a university, this includes materials such as academic journal articles, both preprints and post-prints undergoing peer review, as well as digital versions of thesis and dissertations. It might also include other digital assets generated by academics such as administrative documents, course notes and learning objects. Deposit of material in an institutional repository is sometimes mandated by that institution. Repositories adhere to an internationally-agreed set of technical standards that means that they expose the metadata of each item in their contents on the Web in the same basic way. The contents of all repositories are then indexed by Web search engines such as Google and Google Scholar, creating online Open Access databases of freely-available global research. As the level of self-archiving (the process by which authors deposit their work in repositories) grows the Open Access corpus will represent an increasingly large proportion of the scholarly literature.

DEFINITION OF INSTITUTIONAL REPOSITORIES

Crow (2002) defined institutional repositories as "Digital collections capturing and preserving the intellectual output of a single or multi-university community".

Lynch (2003) defines IRs as "...a university-based institutional repository is a set of services that a university offers to the members of its community for the management and dissemination of digital materials created by the institution and its community members. It is most essentially an organizational commitment to the stewardship of these digital materials, including long-term preservation where appropriate, as well as organization and access or distribution."

NEED OF INSTITUTIONAL REPOSITORIES

The building of an Institutional Repository for any organization is needed in the present scenario of the digital world because of the following certain changes:

- Technological changes;
- Significant increase in the overall volume of research;
- Increasing need for archival and access to unpublished information bearing objects;
- Increasing demand to access knowledge objects from anywhere at any time;
- Increase uncertainty over who will handle the preservation archiving of digital scholarly research materials.

CONTENT TYPES IN INSTITUTIONAL REPOSITORIES

Institutional repository serves as a place to permanently archive research materials in any format such as:

- Previously published materials (articles, book chapters, etc.)

- Conference works and unpublished scholarly works
- Monographs and books
- Peer-reviewed journal articles and conference proceedings
- Theses
- Dissertations
- Lectures
- Research data
- Data files and databases

FEATURES AND BENEFITS OF IRs

An Institutional Repository has the following features and benefits for an institution:

- Centralization and storage of all types of institutional output, including unpublished literature & researcher's work
- Breaking down of publishers' costs and permissions barriers
- Opens up the outputs of the university to the world
- Benefits to researchers and their institutions in terms of prestige, prizes and grant revenue.
- Maximises the visibility and impact of these outputs as a result
- Showcases the university to interested constituencies – prospective staff, students and other stakeholders
- Collects and curates digital outputs
- Manages and measures research and teaching activities
- Enables and encourages interdisciplinary approaches to research
- Facilitates the development and sharing of digital teaching materials and aids
- Supports student endeavours, providing access to theses and dissertations and a location for the development of e-portfolios

- Provides a workspace for work-in-progress, and for collaborative or large-scale projects

INSTITUTIONAL REPOSITORY SOFTWARE

There are a number of open-source software packages available for running an institutional repository including;

- DSpacee (Digital Space)
- E-Prints
- Fedora Commons
- GSDL (Green Stone Digital Library)
- CDSware (CERN Document Server Software)
- ETD-db (Electronic Theses and Dissertations database),
- ARNO
- My Ages (Ages Digital Libraries Software)
- Invenio
- Opus
- MyCoRe
- SobekCM

There are also hosted (proprietary) software services, including:

- Digital Commons, a full-service commercial platform from the Berkeley Electronic Press
- SimpleDL

INSTITUTIONAL REPOSITORY IN LIBRARIES

The Research Library's Role in Digital Repository Services states that "the delivery of repository services is a crucial function of research libraries". Libraries set up repositories to support open access, but also to collect, preserve and provide access to a broad range of content produced by the University and Research community. Libraries can choose from a variety of open source or proprietary software platforms, or have contract with a company to manage their repository for them. Most IRs is organized according to the Disciplinary community and libraries usually work with individual research units to determine collection policies for each community. Building a repository is a fairly simple process for those who have the appropriate technical expertise and the costs of managing an IR are not excessive, involving mainly staffing to maintain the software and promote the repository on campus.

Librarians have critical roles to play in both establishing and maintaining an IR through (Jain, 2009);

Advocacy

Librarians need to know all about the IR, its principles, benefits and operational processes in order to promote it and need to develop advocacy programs, publicise IR through institutional news media and respond to questions by the stakeholders.

Building content

Librarians can employ advocacy and marketing strategies to promote engagement with faculty members and help to generate content. They can also assist by proactively searching for content independently.

Collection administrators and metadata specialists

Librarians have potential roles as collection administrators and metadata specialists. For effective implementation of IR, libraries will need to recruit or train librarians with digital collection management and provide a mediated deposit service for reluctant 'self-archivers'.

Training

Librarians should be able to train staff and students to use the IR and help them prepare their digital products.

Some of the key issues to consider when developing repositories:

- The institutional culture

- The scope of the repository
- Content
- Access levels
- Legal aspects
- Standards
- Sustainability
- Funding

CHALLENGES OF AN INSTITUTIONAL REPOSITORY

Specified challenges for developing IR, scholarly has identified to "...Despite the numerous benefits of an IR, there are implications and potential barriers to its success as summarized below (Jain, 2009):

Cost

The initial financial cost for an open source software adopted by most institutions for creating IRs is not high but the recurrent costs, especially staff costs (e.g. time spent drafting policies, developing guidelines, publicizing, training, supporting users and creating metadata, specialist IT consultancy) may be significant. This is further discussed below.

Difficulties in generating content

A successful IR depends on the willingness of authors to deposit their work voluntarily and there may be local barriers and hindrances to be overcome. There are acknowledged difficulties in generating content, especially at the beginning. Unless the value of an IR can be demonstrated quickly, the organization's long-term commitment to the project may begin to wane. The best way to prove the enduring value of the IR and to ensure its long-term survival is to quickly populate it (Gibbons, 2004).

Sustaining support and commitment

Far too often, it is difficult to sustain continuous support and commitment from the management and academic staff. Lynch (2003) has succinctly described this obstacle: "Stewardship is easy and inexpensive to claim; it is expensive and difficult to honour, and perhaps it will prove to be all too easy to later abdicate". There is a need for institutions to think seriously before launching institutional repository program as it may disintegrate rapidly if not properly managed.

Rights management issues

Sometimes researchers are apprehensive about infringing publishers' copyright and lack adequate awareness about their own intellectual property rights. They may be uncertain about making their work available online before it is published by a traditional publisher.

Working Culture issues

Contributing content to user-generated or 'self-service' sites is time-consuming, and time is something which academics often lack. They may be willing to contribute content but reluctant to do it themselves. This calls for mediated deposits service for them.

Policy related Issues

Experiences suggest that an IR will only function to its capacity when a mandate is in place to populate it but clearly researchers can react negatively to any suggestion of compulsion. Lynch (2003) has cautioned that an IR should not become a tool for enforcing administrative control over academic work.

Lack of incentives

In the absence of any incentive academics feel reluctant to provide even bibliographic details of their scholarly output especially when they know that incentives are available in other institutions."

SOME MAJOR REPOSITORY PROJECTS

There are many national and international repository

initiatives, which aim to enhance the value of individual repositories through content aggregation and the development of common services, such as Dspace repository project (MIT), DRIVER (EU), DRF (Japan), JISC (UK), DARE (Netherlands), HAL (France), CARL IR Program (Canada) and others.

Open Access Repository Directories

Directory of Open Access Repositories (open DOAR) and Registry of Open Access Repositories (ROAR) provides information about the growth and status of repositories throughout the world. Repository makes your research freely and broadly available to a worldwide audience. It uses technology and metadata standards Open Archives Initiative Protocol for Metadata Harvesting (OAI-PMH,) to ensure your works are more findable on the Internet. The Libraries take care to archive and preserve your works for future generations.

Directory of Open Access Repositories (OpenDOAR)

The OpenDOAR provides a quality-assured listing of open access repositories around the world. It harvests and assigns metadata to allow categorisation and analysis to assist the wider use and exploitation of repositories. Each of the repositories has been visited by OpenDOAR staff to ensure a high degree of quality and consistency in the information provided. It is maintained by SHERPA Services, based at the Centre for Research Communications at the University of Nottingham. It is primarily a service to enhance and support the academic and research activities of the global community. OpenDOAR maintains a comprehensive and authoritative list of institutional and subject-based repositories. It also encompasses archives set up by funding agencies like the National Institutes for Health in the USA or the Welcome Trust in the UK and Europe.

Registry of open access repositories (ROAR)

ROAR is a searchable international Registry of Open

Access Repositories indexing the creation, location and growth of open access institutional repositories and their contents. ROAR is part of the EPrints.org network. Its aim is to promote the development of open access by providing timely information about the growth and status of repositories throughout the world. It is hosted at the University of Southampton, UK and made possible by funding from the JISC. Open accesses to research maximize research access and thereby also research impact, making research more productive and effective. http://archives.eprints.org/

THE PRESENT SCENARIO OF OPEN ACCESS INSTITUTIONAL REPOSITORY- WORLDWIDE FRAME

Open Access initiative in worldwide frame identified through a study of the literature and accessed website of "Directory of Open Access Repositories (OpenDOAR)" to get the current information of worldwide contribution to Open access literature in the form figures and tables.

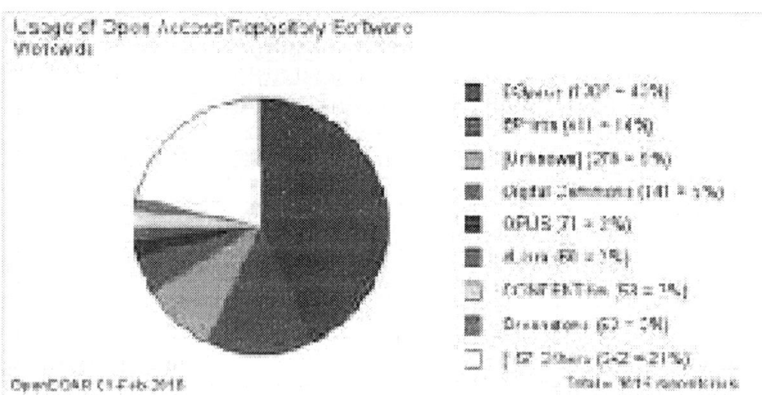

Fig. 1A

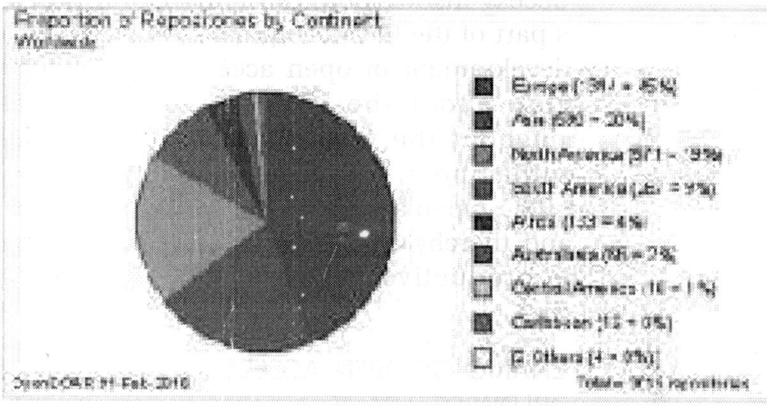
Proportion of Repositories by Continent
Worldwide
Asia
North America
Africa
Australasia
Central America
Caribbean
Others

Fig. 1B

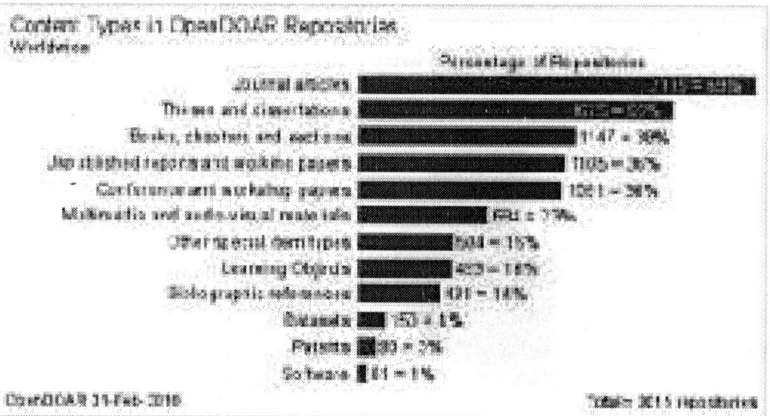
Content Types in OpenDOAR Repositories
Worldwide
Percentage of Repositories
Journal articles
Theses and dissertations
Books, chapters and sections
Conference and workshop papers
Other special item types
Learning Objects
Bibliographic references
Datasets
Patents
Software

Fig. 2A

Subjects in OpenDOAR
Worldwide
Percentage of Repositories
Health and Medicine
Physics and Astronomy
Mechanical Engineering and Materials
Philosophy and Religion
Law and Politics
Psychology

Fig. 2B

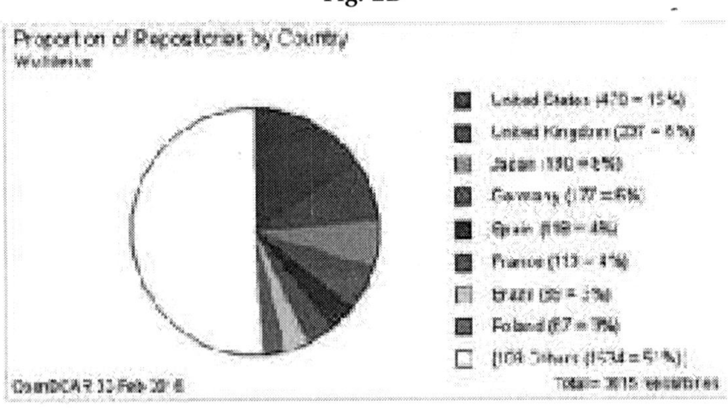
Proportion of Repositories by Country
Worldwide
United States
United Kingdom
Japan
Germany
Spain
France
Brazil
Poland

Fig. 3A

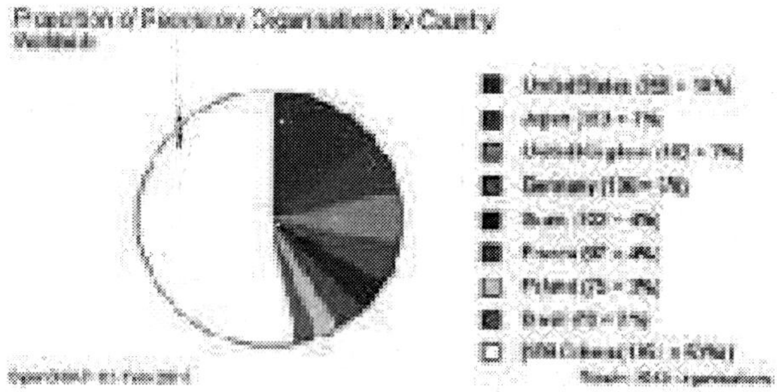

Fig. 3B

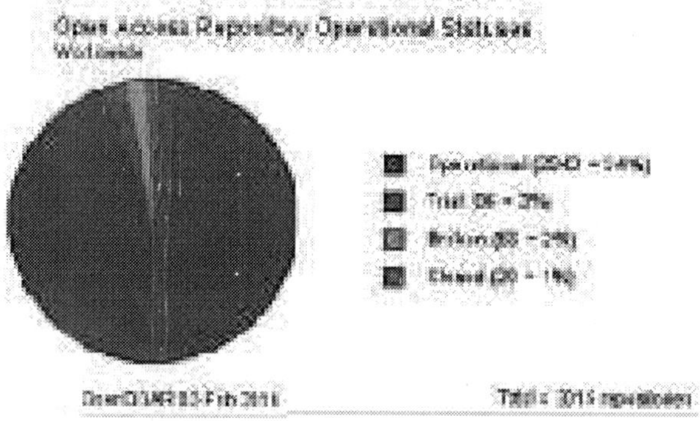

Fig. 4A

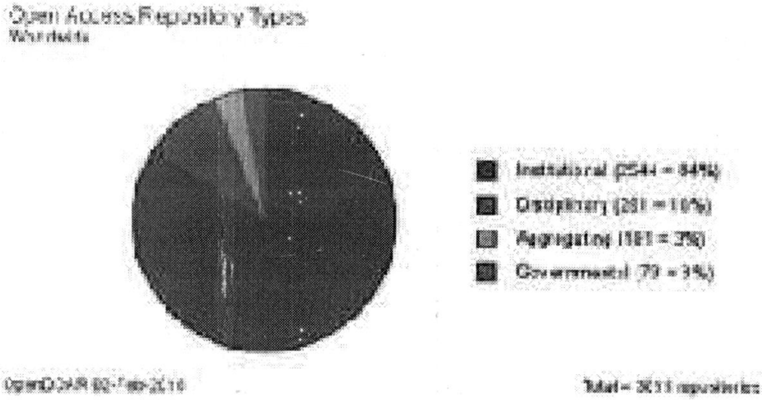

Fig. 4B

Growth and development of the open access Repositories-Worldwide

The exponential growth rate of repositories worldwide as shows in chart1.8(b) it is clear that no of repository increase every year. The chart better represents the true growth in the number of repositories from 2006 onwards. The highest growth in 2012-13(317 repositories) and minimum growth in the year 2013-14(89 repositories only). Shown in chart1.8(a) it is clear that India has moved from some number of repositories prior to the year 2005 and growing every year. The highest growth in 2012-13(12 repositories) followed by in 2006-07(11 repositories) and minimum growth in the year 2014-15(1 repositories only). This significant growth shows that IRs concept and strategically important for institutions, making them a standard for their digital learning initiatives.

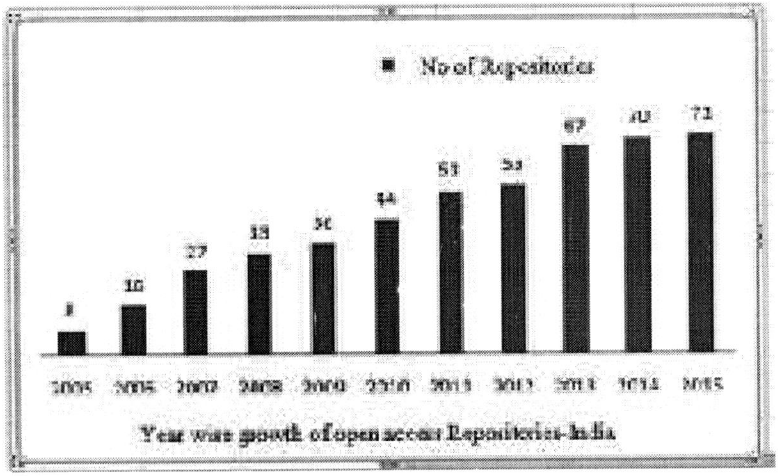

Chart 1.8A

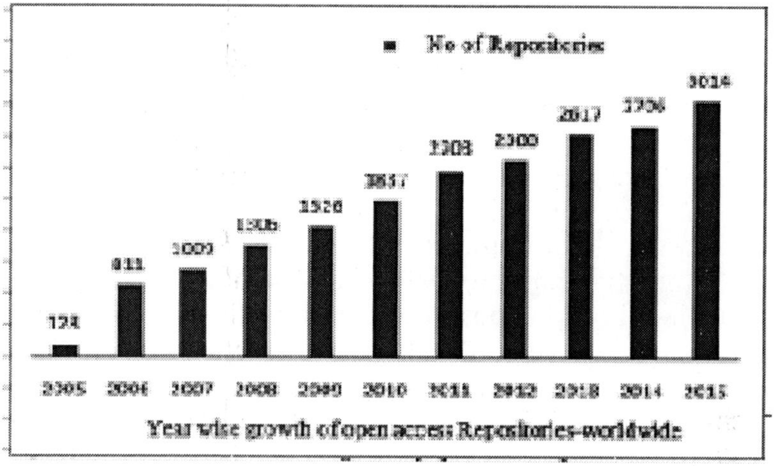

Chart 1.8B

CONCLUSION

Open access is a growing international movement that uses the ICTs to open the doors universal access to information and knowledge in the world. Since the turn of the twenty-first century, there has been a phenomenal increase in the number of open access repositories. It encourages the unrestricted sharing of research results with everyone, everywhere, for the advancement and improvement of science and society. With the global trend, a number of open access repositories have been developed in recent years. India is continuously contributing in Open Access literature as some of the premier institutions, particularly in the science and technology area are providing Open Access to their research publications where 80% of India's repositories are subject-specific and only 20% are multidisciplinary. The most popular IR software platforms DSpace, E-Prints and Greenstone software are used for creating repositories and India's rank 10th position in Directory of Open Access Repositories (OpenDOAR) in terms of number of repositories in the world. Now India becomes an active contributor to global Open Access literature by establishing Open Access archives, institutional repositories, document-specific repositories and subject-specific repositories. In any event, new technologies such as those designed to create IRs can be utilized in far more creative ways to enhance the research endeavor.

REFERENCES

1. Bjo¨rk, B. (2004), "Open access to scientific publications: an analysis of the barriers to change", Information Research,Vol.9No.2, p. 170, available at: http://InformationR.net/ir/92/paper170.html
2. Budapest Open Access Initiative (2002), available at: www.earlham.edu/,peters/fos/boaifaq.htm#openaccess
3. Crow, R. (2002). The case for institutional repositories: a spare position paper, pp.1 -37 , 2002 :The Scholarly Publishing & Academic Resources Coalition.
4. Gibbons, S. (2004). Benefits of an institutional repository. Library Technology Reports, 40(4), 11-16.
5. Lynch, C. (2003). Institutional Repositories: Essential Infrastructure for Scholarship in the Digital Age. ARL, 226, Retrieved 30 Januray, 2016 from http://www.arl.org/bm~doc/br226ir.pdf
6. P. Jain, G. Bentley and M.T. Oladiran , "The role of institutional repository in digital scholarly communications" , Proceedings of African Digital Scholarship & Curation 2009.
7. Pickton, M. & Barwick, J. (2006). A Librarian's guide to institutional repositories. Loughborough University. Retrieved 30 January , 2016 from http://magpie.lboro.ac.uk/dspace/handle/2134/1122

FURTHER READINGS

1. Fayaz Lone, Rafiq Rather, & Gh. Jeelani Shah. (2008). Indian contribution to open access literature: A case study of DOAJ & OpenDOAR. Chinese Librarianship: an International Electronic Journal, 26. URL: http://www.iclc.us/cliej/cl26fayaz.pdf
2. http://archives.eprints.org/
3. http://www.opendoar.org/
4. National Knowledge Commission (2007). Report of the Working Group on Open Access and Open Educational Resources

.available at :http://www.knowledgecommission.gov.in/downloads/documents/wg_open_course.pdf

5. Sawant, S. S. (2013). Past and Present Scenario of Open Access Movement in India. The Journal of Academic Librarianship 39 (2013), 108– 109

9

Facets of Repositories

Tanmay Mondal
Documentation Research and Training Centre,
Bangalore, Karnataka

ABSTRACT

Searching information is not a major problem as information in diverse nature is available on Web. The growth of information in all fields is beyond our prediction. Libraries are still serving leading roles in preserving of all types of information. Digital library has become a part of many organizations to fulfil users' information needs. Digital contents have become a de facto for many of us. Information preservation becomes an important facet in the digital environment. Institutes take care of internal publications which are preserved in an institutional repository. But there are many more repositories other than only institutional based. Publications trend is also changing. Preservation of all those important materials is also important.

Keywords : Digital library, institutional repository, preservation, technologies.

INTRODUCTION

Improvement of communication technologies brings almost each and every aspect of the information on Web. Varieties of information make information more attractive and appropriate in different situations. Information in digital form is increasing rapidly. Electronic information is now cover all aspects of human knowledge such as art, music, medicine, science, movies, videos, books, product literature, newspapers and many more. The library is the place that takes care of all types of information such as text, image, sound, multimedia, datasets, software, audio files, and possibly other as yet unknown types. Traditional library services are gradually moving towards electronic-based services. Modern technology-based services are available in many libraries to fulfil users' requirements. Digital library becomes an inseparable part of any modern library. Repositories are becoming an important storage hub for researched materials to any organization. An institutional repository is a digital library holding the digital output (papers, reports, etc.) of that institution. With the improvement of modern technologies, data is now becoming an important aspect of our information needs. Data preservation has started for its multiple aspects as research data is becoming huge day by day.

TYPES OF LIBRARIES

The library is a non-profit organization that provides an interactive self-paced learning environment. Digital contents fulfill users' information needs. The library has now started providing digital library services which have various aspects that range from a digitized collection of documents to different types information. Library now becomes an environment, which supports the full lifecycle of creation, storage, preservation, dissemination and use of data, information and knowledge (Digital library, 2005). Libraries with different services a are traditional library, automated library, electronic library, digital library and hybrid library.

Traditional library

This kind of library takes care of traditional books, manuscripts, journals, and other sources of recorded information stored within a physical building. The catalogue is used to search library materials. Searching and retrieving materials may not be easy for users. Library documents may not be up to date in many traditional libraries. But this kind of library contains originals documents that may not be available in many modern libraries or in any digital form.

Automated library

Technological advances have presented the opportunity of automating some aspects of traditional libraries (Ogunsola, 2011). The automated library helps library staffs to do their day to day work more efficiently and effectively. A library with the machine-readable catalogue, computerized acquisition, circulation and OPAC (Online Public Access Catalogue) are called as an automated library (Digital library, 2005). Holdings of this type of libraries are same as that of traditional libraries. The implication of technologies in the library has made acquisition, processing, storage, indexing and retrieval of information faster, cheaper and more efficient. The library staffs can use modern communication medium such as E-mail, telephone for answering users' basic queries. Modern libraries are now providing various services through different library automation software.

Electronic library

When automated libraries go for LAN (Local Area Networking) and CD-ROM networking and started procuring E-journal and other similar kind of publication then it is known as an electronic library (Digital library, 2005). It ranges from scanning few pages of documents to linking full-text documents. Full texts are available in CD-ROMs which are provided by publishers. Microfiche, microfilms are also important aspects of an electronic library.

Digital Library

It is a later stage of the electronic library. The majority of the holdings of a digital library is in computer readable form and also acts as a point of access to other sources. It is an interconnected system of systems which includes library's catalogue, digital resources such as e-journals and databases, external resources such as subject portals, library guides, and links to other libraries etc. It is a managed collection of information, with associated services, where the information is stored in digital formats and accessible over a network (as cited in Seadle & Greifeneder, 2007). Some instruments are needed to read an electronic document. It is projected that 1,000 electronic databases/resources are equivalent to 30,000 volumes of printed materials (Ogunsola, 2011). It links to other full-text documents which the library holds access rights.

Hybrid library

The hybrid library is a combination of traditional library and digital library. It is a transitional state between print and digital environment. It is estimated that in near future libraries will be of hybrid nature (Digital library, 2005). The Hybrid library will exist in future as reading habits of us is a mixture of electronic and print documents. The term "hybrid library" was first coined in 1998 by Chris Rusbridge in his article, 'Towards the Hybrid Library' in D-Lib Magazine (Rusbridge, 1998). Most of the present libraries are in hybrid nature.

INSTITUTIONAL REPOSITORY (IR)

Most of the commercial publishers provide subscription-based information. But free access publications are read more and cited more frequently (Lawrence, n.d). Most of these publications come through either by Open Access Journals (OAJ) or by Open Access Archives (OAA). OAA administered by research institutes or any organization (or any entity) for everyone or for a specific community is referred as Institutional Repositories (IRs) (Jayakanth, Minj & Dastidar, 2012). An institutional repository is an archive of digital objects (papers, reports, etc.) of any institution. Many digital publications that are created by the staff members may not be available in any databases (or in any scholarly journals). But those all information may be required for researchers, staffs, students or anyone in future. Institutions need to preserve such digital objects that their staffs create from time to time. More than 3000 IRs are available worldwide listed in the Directory of Open Access Repositories (OpenDOAR, 2006). Institutional Repository (IR) becomes a popular medium for preservation that acts as a central storehouse for digital objects for any organization. Most of the repositories run on digital library management software that are available in the market. DSpace (www.dspace.org) is the leading open source digital library management software.

TYPES OF CONTENTS IN IR

Successful IR depends on its various services that end users use. Services are based on different typed contents (digital objects). Some of the content typed are internal unpublished/published publications, different department's scholarly publications, research results, collaborative project reports, theses/dissertations, preprints (conference publications), post-print (Journal articles), conference presentation, technology reports, newspapers clippings, laboratory research, book chapters, learning objects (including syllabus), images, audio/video materials such as speeches, annual reports, memorandum of understanding, planning sketch (maps), review documents, discussion paper, etc.

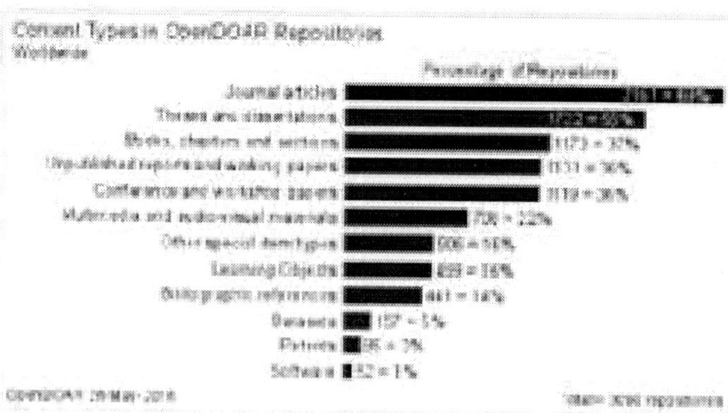

Fig. 1. Content Types in OpenDOAR Repositories Worldwide (Source: OpenDOAR)

TYPES OF REPOSITORIES

The electronic repository is a safe and secure storage place for digital contents. A repository is a storage platform where multiple databases or files are located for distribution over a network. A repository can be a location that is directly accessible to the user without having to travel across a network (repository, n.d). As more and more electronic contents are being created day by day, the importance of preservation gets the first prioritized to the management of any organization. Out of different kinds of repositories, institutional based repositories (84%) are leading as listed in OpenDOAR.

Subject-based repositories (Disciplined Repository)

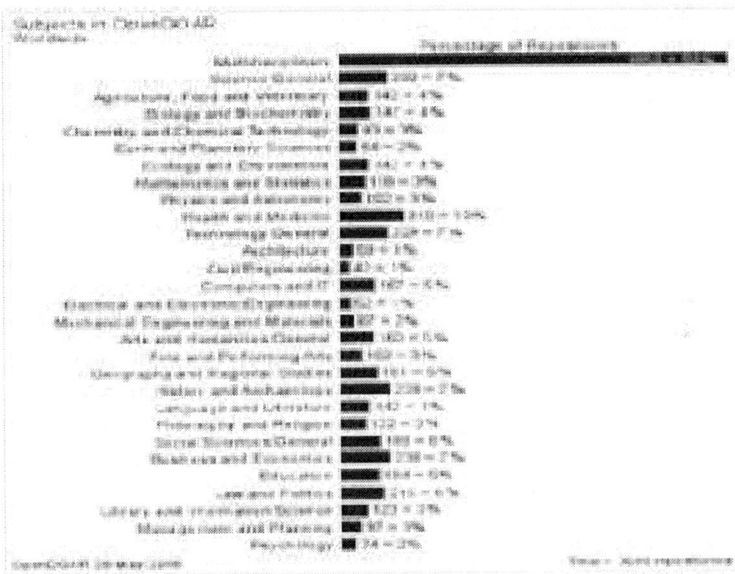

Fig. 2. Subjects in OpenDOAR – Worldwide (Source: OpenDOAR)

Subject-specific repositories preserve documents in a specific domain. It contains most of the important documents in that particular area. First subject specific archive came in 1991 when arXiv (http://arxiv.org/) was started for self-archiving of physics related documents. Most of the subject-specific repositories are in scientific discipline.

Some of the subject-specific repositories are AgEconSearch (research in agricultural and applied economics from the University of Minnesota) (http://ageconsearch.umn.edu/), ERIC (Education Resources Information Center) (https://eric.ed.gov/), Librarians' Digital Library (library and information science) (www.drtc.isibang.ac.in/ldl) hosted by Documentation Research and Training Centre. List of discipline oriented repositories are listed in Open Access Directory (OAD) (Disciplinary repositories, n.d). Subject specific repositories shown in OpenDOAR are shown in Fig. 2.

Aggregator repositories (Multidisciplinary Repository)

It collects data from several repositories. The idea behind aggregator repositories is to expose various kinds of contents that can be easily accessed in one platform. Mainly publishers provide various resources in their centralized search platform. EBSCO (founded in 1986) (http://search.ebscohost.com/) is one of the largest aggregators. Other important aggregator platforms are ProQuest (http://www.proquest.com/), JSTOR (http://www.jstor.org/), ACM digital library (http://dl.acm.org/) and many more. More than 3.3% repositories are this kind of repositories (OpenDOAR, 2006). Some of the aggregator repositories are internet archive (https://archive.org/), NISCAIR's Online Periodicals Repository (NOPR) (http://nopr.niscair.res.in/), Indus(http://drtc1.isibang.ac.in/indus/), Washington Research Library Consortium (WRLC) (http://www.wrlc.org/), Indian Council for Agricultural Research (ICAR) (http://www.icar.org.in/), BASE (https://www.base-search.net), Zenodo (https://zenodo.org/), The Biodiversity Heritage Library (BHL) (http://biodivlib.wikispaces.com/), edX (https://www.edx.org/) etc.

Institutional Repository (Research Repository)

This kind of repository is important as it preserves important documents which may not be available in many commercial platforms. Some of the institutional based repositories are DSpace@MIT (https://dspace.mit.edu/), e-prints in library & information science (http://eprints.rclis.org/), eScholarship (http://escholarship.org/), Institutional Repository of the University of Pretoria (http://repository.up.ac.za/), ePrints@IISc (http://eprints.iisc.ernet.in/), DSpace at Indian Institute of Management Kozhikode (http://dspace.iimk.ac.in/), institutional repository of IIT Bombay (http://dspace.library.iitb.ac.in/jspui/), Mahatma Gandhi University Theses Online (http://www.mgutheses.org/) etc. Some of the repositories a e either available freely or restricted to a specific community. These repositories are mainly for preservation of scholarly publications which come from faculty members, students, staffs and other community members and usually, it is maintained by the library staffs.

National repository (Governmental Repository)

The national repository is like a national record keeper that provides different services to all. It is mainly a Government initiative that takes care of such repositories. Some of them are National Archives and Records Administration (NARA) (https://www.archives.gov/about/), DigitalNZ (http://www. digitalnz.org/), Digital Public Library of America (https://dp.la/), National Digital Library (https://ndl.iitkgp.ac.in/index.php) etc. The Government of India has started DigiLocker (https://digilocker.gov.in/about.php) that is a platform for issuance and verification of documents and certificates in a digital way that citizens can access anytime, anywhere.

Some of the other repositories listed in Registry of Open Access Repositories (ROAR) are research cross-institutional, research data, open and linked data, learning and teaching objects, demonstration, web observatory, and others.

Data repository

Data can come in many forms that can be used for many purposes. One of the immerging repositories is data repository. Data Repository is a logical (and sometimes physical) partitioning of data where multiple databases which apply to specific applications or sets of applications reside (What is Data Repository, 2008). Research data is mainly collected, observed, or created in a digital form, for purposes of analyzing to produce original research results. Some of the data repositories are Edinburgh DataShare (http://datashare.is.ed.ac.uk/), agINFRA (http://aginfra.eu/), food and agriculture organization of the united nations (http://faostat3.fao.org/home/E), figshare (https://figshare.com/), Open Government Data (OGD) Platform India (https://data.gov.in/), registry of research data repository (http://www.re3data.org/), DataONE Search (http://search.dataone.org), China Data Online (http://chinadataonline.org/), OECD iLibrary (http://www.oecd-ilibrary.org/), Inter-university Consortium for Political and Social Research (ICPSR) (http://www.icpsr.umich.edu/icpsrweb/landing.jsp), Databrary (https://nyu.databrary.org) and many more. The future preservation policies would be around data repository.

CONCLUSION

There are legacy resources (largely non-digital resources) like manuscript, maps, hand written letters, etc., which serve a large number of patrons in a traditional library. Technologies brought digital contents that come from many sources. The library doesn't hold any right on digital contents except access rights. Maintaining access right is also not an easy job as it depends on many factors (library budget, subscription rate increases, maintenance of technologies, etc.). Again users requirements are to be well supported by incorporating newer services like e-books, e-journal. The future library is going to be technology based that must incorporate traditional library services with the help of modern technologies. Repositories will be the medium for accessing most of the resources from the Web. Knowing right repositories for our information needs will help a lot to retrieve important documents.

REFERENCES

1. Digital library. (2005). In LISWiki. Retrieved May 6, 2016, from http://liswiki.org/wiki/Digital_library.
2. Disciplinary repositories, (n.d).http://oad.simmons.edu/oadwiki/Disciplinary_repositories
3. Figure 1. Content Types in OpenDOAR Repositories Worldwide. Retrieved May26, 2016, from http://www.opendoar.org/onechart-legacy.php?cID=&ctID=&rtID=&clID=&lID=&potID=&rSoftWareName=&search=&groupby=ct.ctDefinition&orderby=Tally%20DESC& charttype=bar &width=600&caption=Content%20Types%20in %20Open DOAR%20Repositories%20-%20Worldwide.
4. Figure 2. Subjects in OpenDOAR – Worldwide from OpenDOAR. Retrieved May 26, 2016, from http://www.opendoar.org/onechart-legacy.php?cID=&ctID=&rtID=&clID=&lID=&potID=&rSoftWareName =&search=& groupby=cl.clTitle&orderby=cl.clCode&charttype=bar&width=600&caption=Subjects%20in%20OpenDOAR%20-%20Worldwide.
5. Jayakanth, F., Minj , F &Dastidar, P. G. (2012). Setting up an open access digital repository: A case study, Annals of Library and Information Studies, 59(1) 16-24.
6. Lawrence, S. (n.d). Free online availability substantially increases a paper's impact, Nature: Webdebates. Retrieved March 11, 2016, from http://www.nature.com/nature/debates/e-access/Articles/lawrence.html
7. Ogunsola, L. A. (2011). The Next Step in Librarianship: Is The Traditional Library Dead?.Library Philosophy and Practice (e-journal), Paper 606. Retrieved from http://digitalcommons.unl.edu/libphilprac/606.
8. OpenDOAR, (2006). Retrieved May 23, 2016, from http://www.opendoar.org/.
9. Repository, (n.d). Retrieved May 1, 2016, from http://www.webopedia.com/TERM/R/repository.html.
10. Rusbridge, C. (1998). Towards the Hybrid Library. D-Lib Magazine. Retrieved May10, 2016, from http://www.dlib.org/dlib/july98/rusbridge/07rusbridge.html.
11. Registry of Open Access Repositories. (2003). Retrieved May 23, 2016, from http://roar.eprints.org/.
12. Seadle, M &Greifeneder, E. (2007). Defining a digital library.

Library Hi Tech, 25(2), 169-173. Doi: http://dx.doi.org/10.1108/07378830710754938.

13. What is Data Repository, (2008).GreekInterview. Retrieved April 10, 2016, from http://www.learn.geekinterview.com/data-warehouse/dw-basics/what-is-data-repository.html.

10

Green Library : A Need of Time

Shaveta

Assistant Librarian, Amardeep Singh Shergill College, (A Constituent College of Guru Nanak Dev University, Amritsar) Mukandpur, Distt. SBS Nagar, Panjab.

ABSTRACT

The paper deals with the concept of Green library. Its need and standards at global and national level for constructing a Green library like LEED, IGBC ASHRAE, BREEM etc discussed. It also gives a light on Green Libraries at national and international levels. Tips for converting the present building into sustainable and green library building are also given.

Keywords : Green Library, Sustainable, LEE, Green Library Building, Energy Saver, Eco-Friendly.

INTRODUCTION

As we know that Global Warming is a very serious issue these days. Increasing the number of Industries, continuing cutting of trees and forests, etc has affected the environment. The result is air pollution, water pollution, sound pollution etc. In simple words, our earth is going to be polluted. To save our earth we must be aware and change our habits, our lifestyle to come over the problem of Global Warming. We must aware with the concept of "Go Green" and "Sustainability". It is a contribution towards maintaining the natural ecological balance in the environment and preserving the planet and its natural system and resources. It is a great effort by us to protect natural resources for our coming generation.

The library is a reflection of a society. Here libraries and librarian can play a vital role in this worldwide phenomenon because libraries are a knowledge house and always disseminate information and Librarian is information providers. They can organize seminars, competition, debate and lecture to aware the users about pollution and can tell the need and importance of the eco-friendly environment. Librarian can also convert their Libraries into Green Libraries. Green Library is not a new concept in libraries. In past, during construction of the library building, architectures must keep in mind how to provide proper sunlight, natural air, ventilate in library hall because rare books, manuscripts need a special temperature to protect them from insects. Some indoor plants are also placed there to give a pleasant environment so that users can stay for long hours in the library.

MEANING AND DEFINITION OF TERMS

Go Green

- According to The Online Slang Dictionary, Go Green Means to change one's lifestyle for the safety and benefit of the environment.
- According to World Reference.Com's Online Language Dictionary, Go Green means make environmentally-friendly choices.
- The US Chamber of Commerce Small Business Nation Defines Going Green as simply taking steps to, Conserve Energy, Reduce Pollution and Save Money.

Sustainability

- According to Merriam Webster Dictionary, Sustainability means involving methods that do not completely use up or destroy natural resources.

- According to Oxford Dictionary, Sustainability is conserving an ecological balance by avoiding depletion of natural resources.

WHAT ARE GREEN LIBRARIES?

The word Green in itself says that an eco-friendly library the term GREEN can be defined as;

G – Growing,

E–Ecology,

E–Economy,

R – Reusing,

N- Naturally.

The California Integrated Waste Management Board defines a green or sustainable building as, "a structure that is designed, built, renovated, operated, or reused in an ecological and resource-efficient manner." (Antonelli, 2008) According to Report to California's Sustainable Building Task Force Green or Sustainable building use key resources like energy, water, materials and land much more efficiently than a building that is simply built to code. They also create healthier work, learning and living environment with more natural light and cleaner air and contribute to improved employee and student health, comfort and productivity. Sustainable buildings are cost-effective, saving taxpayer dollars by reducing operations and maintenance costs, as well as by lowering utility bills. (Kats, 2003)

NEED OF THE GREEN LIBRARIES

Green Library is need of the time. To save our earth and natural resources for our future generation we must have to change our lifestyle. To reduce the impact of Global Warming on us we needed to generate Green Buildings/ Green Libraries. The need of the green libraries is discussed as:

- Budget in the construction of Green Library is not a

problem. It is an affordable project.

- To reduce the energy and water consumption
- To enhance the indoor air quality.
- Green Library is needed to provide an eco-friendly, healthy environment for students, scholars and employees.
- Green Libraries Building can also encourage others to convert their department buildings into green buildings.
- Green Library reduce the carbon footprints i.e. carbon dioxide.
- Green Library is very economic because in Green Library we mostly use Natural air and Natural Light so it reduces the bill of electricity.
- Green Library is very cost effective

HOW TO BUILD A GREEN LIBRARY

Leadership in Energy and Environment Design (LEED) has described five things which must be kept in mind while designing the Green Libraries. These Five categories are discussed as;

Site Location

Selection of site Building is a very important part of constructing Green Library. LEED gives many suggestions for site selection process. According to LEEDs guidelines, library should be situated in the heart of the city, in heavily populated area. So that people can consult the library easily. They can use public transport or can reach on foot or by two-wheelers. The parking area should be cover with natural shading or green roofs to reduce the heat effect.

Water Conservation

The World has changed. There is less amount of drinking water on earth so we should stop wastage of water. LEED says Libraries should conserve water and rainwater should use for garden harvesting around the building. Preference must be given to using waterless urinals.

Energy Efficiency

Energy efficiency means using less energy to provide the same service. LEED gives heaviest weighted to Energy Efficiency. Energy can be conserved with the natural way and with the help of technology. It can be known as Passive and Active strategy. The passive strategy could be using sunlight and natural air, using public transport or car pool to save fuel. The active strategy includes using of advanced technology to save energy like use of LED light, Fluorescent Light, Solar energy, using of Laptop or Ultrabooks instead of computers to save electricity.

Building Material

The material selection in construction and designing of a building is a big issue. Some things which must keep in mind during the selection of building material are;

- Affordable
- Locally Available
- Reusable
- Maximum Energy Saver
- Low or Non-Toxic
- Moisture Resistant
- Durable
- Enhanced Indoor Air Quality Etc.

Indoor Air Quality (IAQ)

Indoor Air Quality is very important part of Green Building. To avoid air pollution inside the building, Indoor plantation can be done. Green Buildings reduce IAQ problem by providing good ventilation and Installing exhaust system for fresh air. In Green Library building low or no VOC (Volatile Organic Compound) paint or eco-friendly paint is used. Green Library Building acts as a safeguard for its users and workers.

STANDARDS FOR GREEN LIBRARIES

International Standards for Green Building

During Construction or renovation of building harmful chemicals or material is used which affect the human health and building. Standards of constructing Green Building decide the negative impact of building on the environment. The main aim of Standards, Certifications, and Rating System is promoting the construction of Green Buildings around us. Some Major Standards, Codes are discussed below:

USGBC Standards (http://in.usgbc.org/leed#rating) : Leadership in Energy and Environment Design (LEED) is recognized standards for measuring building sustainability. The version 4 is the latest version of LEED which is introduced in 2014. LEED was developed by The United States Green Building Council (USGBC) in 2000; USGBC is a non-profit organization of The United States. LEED rating system is based on points level: Certified (40-49 points), Silver (50-59 points), Gold (60-79points) and Platinum (80+ points) these points and level are decided on the bases of six major components, these are - 1. Site Location, 2. Water Conservation, 3. Energy Efficiency, 4. Material and Resources, 5. Indoor Quality, 6. Innovation and Design Process.

The LEED certification process is designed to promote to save the natural resource that is better for our environment and health.

Energy Star Rating System (https://www.energystar.gov/) : Energy Star Rating System is created by the U.S. EPA and DOE that uses benchmarking methods to assess a building's energy and water use. Every year Energy Star Award is given to organizations for achievement in helping to improve energy efficiency.

The Harvard Green Building Standards (https://green.harvard.edu) : The 2014 latest version of the standards includes the maximum use of eco-friendly and reusable building material which has zero side effects on human health and environment. It also includes a requirement for

LEED v4 Gold Certification and revision to Measurement and Verification standards for the effectiveness of energy and mechanical system.

BREEM (http://www.breeam.com/) : Building Research Establishment Environmental Assessment Method (BREEM) was launched in 1990. It is the oldest green building rating system used by 77 countries. There are more than 549,699 BREEM certified developments and 2,250,980 buildings are registered under BREEM.

ASHRAE (https://www.ashrae.org) : American Society of Heating, Refrigerating and Air-Conditioning Engineers (ASHRAE) is a global leader in the arts and sciences of heating, ventilation, air conditioning and refrigeration. The important ASHRAE standards are:

55 : Thermal Comfort

62.1 : Indoor Air Quality

90.1 : Building Energy Conservation

135 : BACnet (Building Automation and Control)

189.1 : High Performance of Green Buildings

National Standards for Green Building

IGBC Indian Green Building Council Standards (www.igbc.in) : The Indian Green Building Council (IGBC), part of the Confederation of Indian Industry (CII) was formed in the year 2001. The vision of the council is, to enable a sustainable built environment for all and facilitate India to be one of the global leaders in the sustainable built environment by 2015. The council is Committee-Based, Member-Driven and Consensus-Focused. Till date, it has 1,959 members (143 Founding Members) and 3,774 projects are registered under IGBC. IGBC is licensed with LEED from the US Green Building Council untill June 2018. The various levels of rating awarded are as below:

Certification Level	*Owner Occupied Building*	*Tenant Occupied Building*	*Recognition*
Certified	50-59	50-59	Good Practice
Silver	60-69	60-69	Best Practice
Gold	70-79	70-79	Outstanding Performance
Platinum	80-89	80-89	National Excellence
Super Platinum	90-100	90-100	Global Leadership

GRIHA – Green Rating for Integrated Habitat Assessment (http://www.grihaindia.org/) : GRIHA Council promotes scientific and administrative issues related to the sustainable habits in the Indian subcontinent. GRIHA was founded in 2007 by TERI (The Energy and Resources Institute, New Delhi) with support from MNRE (Ministry of New and Renewable Energy, Government of India) GRIHA developed a rating system which was adopted by all types of Green buildings. The GRIHA Council has signed MoU with NASA to promote the green building concepts together. The GRIHA Trophy is given in the annual function organized by NASA so that students of architecture can be encouraged and motivate towards the sustainable buildings. GRIHA Council also conducts awareness programme, workshop, training programme on green buildings and GRIHA rating system. .To make the information readily accessible and available, GRIHA Council has started a "Series of Webinar"

Bureau of Energy Efficiency (https://beeindia.gov.in): The Government of India has set up Bureau of Energy Efficiency (BEE) on 1st March 2002, under the provisions of the Energy Conservation Act, 2001. For buildings, BEE has its own rating system based on 1 to 5 star scales. More stars mean more energy efficiency. The RBI, Delhi and Bhubaneswar are examples of 5 star rating buildings.

SOME MAJOR GREEN LIBRARIES

Green Libraries at International Level

Fayetteville Public Libraries, USA is First building in Arkansas to applied LEED. It has many green techniques used in the reading room, circulation counter and in other parts of library the building.

Scattle Central Library, USA has applied many green techniques like rainwater is collected over roof and used for irrigation.

Minneapolis Public Library, USA is an example of reducing rainwater runoff, heat and cooling load. Here rooftop is planted with the vegetation to reduce the temperature of the building.

University of California, Merced Kolligan Library, USA was awarded LEED's Certificate in 2007. University uses mostly recycle material and building material used for its construction is mostly locally available.

National Library, Singapore library is the greenest building on the planet. It is designed with light shelves through which light filter into the library without having bad effects.

Green Libraries at National Level

Anna Centenary Library is a state of the art library building from Department of Public Libraries, Tamil Nadu State Government. The prestige building achieved LEED Gold rating under new construction by Indian Green Building Council (IGBC)

Perma Karpo Library is the best example of sustainable building. It is designed by Arup for White Lotus School in a small village of Ladahk (in the Indian Himalayas).

Mumbai University Library Building of Mumbai University in Vidyanagri Campus in Kalina is based on the concept of green building.

SUGGESTIONS TO CONVERT LIBRARIES INTO GREEN LIBRARIES

Green libraries are most important need of the time to save the earth. It reduces cost, energy and wastage of natural resources. Instead of constructing a new green building with some small efforts, with awareness, we can convert existing library building into green library. The steps to convert the normal building into green building are given as:

- Maximum use of natural light.
- Use of window for air
- Grow more plants around the building
- Use eco-friendly cleaners.
- Save rainwater for irrigation of garden around the building.
- Stop wastage of Water.
- Use of eco-friendly paints.
- Use of laptop to save electricity than desktop version.
- Switch off the lights and fans when it is not required.
- Use CFL and LED bulb instead of tube light and other bulbs.
- Use network printer instead of personal printer.
- Use of E-books and e-journals can save paper.
- Digital library saves papers.
- Re-fill toner cartridges instead of buying new.
- Prefer to solar equipment.
- Use of low flow faucet and toilets to conserve water.
- Use public transport to save fuel and avoid air pollution.
- Use recycled products.
- Say No to Plastic Bags.
- Encourage employees to car pool.
- Buy locally available products.

- Use Energy Star products to save energy.
- Use roof garden to control the heat of the building.

There are many other steps which are helpful in converting to green building. We must have to aware of it. College, Universities must organize seminars and lecture to aware the students and people about the eco-friendly environment.

CONCLUSION

Green Libraries play a paramount role towards the welfare of mankinds. Green libraries do not requirc a high budget for constructions and maintenance. Only awareness is important to build an eco-friendly building. The library is a great place to educate the people. So librarian should take initiatives to aware the people about eco-friendly lifestyle. Green Library Building concept in India is not so popular. So, college, Universities, and Institutions should organize seminars, awareness programmes, lectures to aware the people about sustainable and eco-friendly buildings. Environment agencies and government should organize conferences, workshops for awareness of this new concept and grants should be given for constructing Green Library Buildings.

REFERENCES

1. Antonelli,Monika(2008) The Green library movement : An overview of green library literature and actions from 1979 to the future of green libraries Retrieved from https://green.nd.edu/assets/24828/escholarship_uc_item_39d3v236.pdf accessed on 6/9/2016
2. Enck , Corey(2013)New Ways to Save Water in LEED v4 Retrieved From http://greencleanguide.com/three-primary-rating-systems-for-green-buildings-in-india/ accessed on 5/9/2016
3. Kats ,Greg (2003)The Costs and Financial Benefits of Green Buildings. A Report to California's Sustainable Building Task Force Retreived from http://www.usgbc.org/Docs/Archive/General/Docs1992.pdf accessed on 7/9/2016
4. Pangail, Ramyia Krishnan(2015) Green Libraries: Meaning,

Standards and Practices. Episteme: an online interdisciplinary , multidisciplinary and multi-cultural journal. Bharat College of Arts and Commerce ,. Badlapur. Vol 4(3). Pp. 1-9 Retrieved from http://www.episteme.net.in/phocadownloadpap/userupload/december2015/articles/1-green%20library-updated2.pdf accessed on 7/9/2016

5. http://in.usgbc.org/leed#rating
6. http://in.usgbc.org/sites/default/files/LEED%20v4%20BDC_04.05.16_current.pdf
7. http://indianexpress.com/ 17 October 2014
8. http://me.hku.hk/bse/bee-sbd/150324_ASHRAE-ACRA_Talk_189.1_90.pdf
9. http://www.breeam.com/
10. http://www.calrecycle.ca.gov/greenbuilding/materials/
11. http://www.colapublib.org/sustain/
12. http://www.delhijalboard.nic.in/djbdocs/consumer/conservation.htmf
13. http://www.greenbuilding.com/knowledge-base/indoor-air-quality
14. http://www.greenbusinesscentre.com/site/ciigbc/greenbuild.jsp?servid=184667
15. http://www.greenlibraries.org/usa_green_libraries_directory_a_-_g
16. http://www.ifla.org/past-wlic/2011/196-wang-en.pdf
17. http://www.slideshare.net/baburajiv2007/leed-india-case-study-cii-sohrabji-godrej-itc-green-center?next_slideshow=1
18. http://www.urbandictionary.com/define.php?term=Go%20green
19. http://www.usgbc.org/articles/new-ways-save-water-leed-v4 accessed on 8/9/2016
20. http://www.wordreference.com/es/translation.asp? tranword=go%20green
21. https://beeindia.gov.in/
22. https://en.wikipedia.org/wiki/Green_building_in_India
23. https://green.harvard.edu/topics/green-buildings/green-building-standards
24. https://igbc.in/igbc/
25. https://igbc.in/igbc/html_pdfs/abridged/IGBC%20Green%20New %20Buildings%20Rating% 20System%20 (Version%203.0).pdf

26. https://igbc.in/igbc/redirectHtml.htm?redVal=showLeednosign

27. https://www.ashrae.org/resources—publications/bookstore/standard-189-1

28. https://www.coa.gov.in/show_img.php?fid=150

29. https://www.ibi.hu-berlin.de/de/studium/studprojekte/buchidee/bi12/bobcatsss_2013_designing-the-green-library.pdf

30. https://www.newworldencyclopedia.org/entry/Green_library

31. https://www.sla.org/wp-content/uploads/2015/06/1486_HotTopicsinArchitectBldgDsgnArzeta.pdf

32. https://www.thebalance.com/understanding-the-leed-certification-basics-844729?utm_term=standards+for+green+libraries&utm_content=p1-main-3-title&utm_medium=sem-sub&utm_source=google_s&utm_campaign=adid-29f20ee9-f728-4257-b456-e4c2a1981120-0-ab_gsb_ocode-4573&ad=semD&an=google_s&am=broad&q=standards+for+green+libraries&o=4573&qsrc=1&l=sem&askid=29f20ee9-f728-4257-b456-e4c2a1981120-0-ab_gsb

33. onlineslangdictionary.com/meaning-definition-of/go-green

34. www.igbc.in

35. http://en.wikipedia.org/wiki/Green_library.

11

Green Computing and Its Implementation in Library and Information Centers : A New Color to Go Green & Step toward Green Library

Jayshri Mondal
Librarian, Govt. R P S PG College,
Baikunthpur, Korea, C.G.

ABSTRACT

During recent years, attention toward 'Green computing' has moved research trends to search for energy-saving techniques for computing equipment. Green computing is computing in environmentally sustainable manner where one could use different strategies to reduce carbon footprint and energy consumption and also for e-waste management. It is not only beneficial for our environment but also for e-waste management. It not only beneficial for our environment but also for cost efficiency of our institution. Library as a social institution represents society and ICT equipment are pervasive in library and information centers now a day, for providing better services. So libraries can implement the green computing as social responsibility, to save our environment and reduce energy consumption and cut cost by refurbishing equipment. This paper discusses the ways and technologies that how we can implement green practices in our daily life as well as in library and information centers.

Keywords : Green computing, need of green computing, ways to implement green computing, energy efficiency, e-waste management.

INTRODUCTION

Green is a new color of computing, which ensures efficient utilization of computing resources by reducing carbon footprint, wastage of electricity, and increasing power efficiency, efficient running of the organization by cost reduction and maximum benefit. Now a day library also uses computing resources for providing better services so as a library and information professional a major role can be played by us toward efficiency in everyday work and to contribute in saving our mother earth. Libraries as a social institution reflect society so awareness, green purchasing, rating of energy efficiency, energy saving and cost reduction are main areas of concern. Green computing is designing, manufacturing, use and disposal of computing resources in a green way.

Green computing as a buzzword gains popularization in last few years when it comes in consideration for environmental sustainability because computing resources also somewhat contribute to global warming also its hazardous toxicity creates a threat to environment, the disposal of computing peripherals are also known as e-waste is major problem in front of us because only small amount of such e-wastes are actually going for recycling and are non biodegradable. Power consumption is also a major concern because computing needs electricity. A big step to tackle the issue is energy star rating which ensures power efficiency and reduction of usage of electricity by green design and manufacturing. There is also less awareness about green computing existing in society.

AIMS AND OBJECTIVES

- To discuss green computing in general scenario.
- To discuss the need to follow green way to computing in library and information centers.
- To discuss the ways to implement green computing in libraries and information centers.

DIFFERENT ISSUES OF GREEN COMPUTING AND LIS PROFESSIONALS

The whole computing product life cycle is centering around the phases of design, manufacture, use and disposal so Green computing is pervasive for all of these phases:

Design green

Designing energy efficient and environmentally sound components, computers, servers, cooling Equipment, and data centers.

Manufacturing green

Manufacturing electronic components, computers, and other associated subsystems with minimal impact on the Environment.

Use in green way

Reducing the energy consumption of computers and other information systems as well as using them in an environmentally sound manner.

Dispose in green way

Refurbishing and reusing old computers and properly recycling unwanted computers and other electronic equipment.

In this, whole Product Life cycle, Library and information centers can contribute in third and fourth phase which are, use and dispose. By using certain techniques and technologies of green computing and by creating awareness in society about a greenish way to move forward with computing, libraries can contribute. By taking some small steps like shutting down the computers when not in use, power off the monitor while simply downloading, and prefer virtualization libraries can save a lot of their valuable money.

NEED TO GO GREEN IN LIBRARY AND INFORMATION CENTERS

This is true that green computing has many advantages for environmental sustainability but it also has many advantages for us.

Green computing for saving cost

Green computing saves our lot of money by reducing the amount in bill payment by lower electricity consumption and also by recycling or refurbishing the old computing devices.

Green computing for environment sustainability

Green computing reduces carbon footprint also reduces the use hazardous component as mercury, lead and instead using biodegradable substances such as bamboo or non-hazardous material.

Lower energy consumption

New green manufacturing processes lead to target of lower energy consumption by replacing the old energy-sucking displays to LED or LCD based displays.

Social responsibility

As being a part of the society we all have a responsibility toward our environment, society and our planet.

HOW TO IMPLEMENT GREEN COMPUTING

The way actually can be adopted for going toward total green is largely concern of management. Phases of implementation include:

- Planning

- Implementing
- Reviewing

In this paper, we discuss implementation phase.

Here we discuss some of the ways to implement green computing in library and information centers are:

Wi-Fi Scheduler : It is an easy way to control the timely ON and OFF of wireless network, it is a very useful way to save battery life during your busy and rest hours.

Power Saving by reducing Cable Length : How long the cable will be it emits such amount of energy because of the bigger surface area.

Power Saving by Hard Drives Hibernation : Hard drive hibernation allows you to shut everything down by copying all the information from RAM to Hard drive.

Power Saving by Standby Mode : Same as hibernation but the difference is that allows memory not to be shut down.

Green Laptops : Bamboo laptop, paper laptop are newer laptop with the same durability but as it made up of biodegradable material it gives it an innovative touch.

Smaller sized monitor : smaller sized monitor takes less amount of electricity as compared to bigger sized monitor also LCD and LED are more energy efficient than CRT monitors.

Green surfing : By green browsing practices, green google, yahoo and firefox can be implemented through a website named Blackle.com may reduce power consumption during surfing by providing black background.

Using a different kind of scheduler or awakening technology : As we already discuss wi-fi scheduler, some other kind of schedulers can be used like Wake On LAN (WOL), Time based Power Over Ethernet (POE).

Purchase energy rated material : Energy star rating is emerged as a initiative in this direction energy star's number shows energy efficiency of product so before purchasing we have to check out for this.

Reduce paper consumption by using various technologies : Papers increases the carbon footprint enormously so by using different technologies we should reduce its consumption like cloud computing, virtualization, consolidation and optimization etc.

Refurbishing parts of computer : Up gradation can also be done to utilize old one in a new way.

- Create awareness about green computing by different types of publication and recommend it to include in the curriculum.
- Turn off the computer when not in use.
- When there are any activities such as installation or downloading turn off the monitor because monitors suck a huge amount of electricity.
- Implementing cloud computing.
- **Purchase LCD or LED monitor :** LCD (Liquid crystal display) or LED (Light emitting diode) consumes less electricity than CRT also they put less stress on eyes so this should be preferred.
- Buy vegetable or non-petroleum-based inks
- Recycle things as much possible- Only very few e-waste (unused parts of computers or other electronic devices) truly goes for recycling, It sometimes creates a panic that this will be managed so recycling is a help in this.
- Virtualization and optimization.

CONCLUSION

Green computing pervades its steps for environmental sustainability and is much thruster area which needs proper consideration because environment threats make this necessary to give it proper consideration and as a library and information science professional we have a social responsibility to make people aware. Also to run library and information centers efficiently it helps us to cut cost and increase energy efficiency. Green computing has the very vast scope it can be implemented in all the phases including design, manufacturing, use and then disposal.

REFERENCES

1. Pant, A., and Moorthy, A.L, "Knowledge Management and safeguarding Indian Traditional Knowledge". Annals of Library and Information Studies. 60, p.88-97. (2013).
2. Maan, N.K. and Dhillon, N.K, "GREEN: The New Color in Computer Technology". IJCSMC, Vol. 2, Issue. 6, June 2013, pg.156–162. ISSN 2320–088X.
3. Jadhwani, D., Agrawal, M. and Mande, H, "Study of Efficient Utilization of Power using green Computing". International Journal of Advanced Computer Research ISSN (print): 2249-7277 Volume-2 Number-4 Issue-6 December-2012.
4. Dheer, R., "Green computing – The New Era of Energy Efficient Computing". International Journal of Computers & Technology ISSN: 2277-3061 Volume 3, No. 1, AUG, 2012.
5. Sheikh, R.A., Lanjewar, U.A., "Green Computing- Embrace a Secure Future". International Journal of Computer Applications (0975 – 8887) Volume 10– N.4, November 2010.
6. Microsoft: Green IT taking the first step (2010) Retrieved from http://www.microsoft.com/environment/our_commitment/articles/green_guide.aspx
7. http://www.theglobalwarmingstatistics.org/globalwarming-essays
8. Green Computing ,http://en.wikipedia.org/wiki/Green_computing
9. Bamboo Laptops, http://event.asus.com/notebook/bamboo/, 2008
10. Lenovo thinkpad Laptops, http://shopap.lenovo.com/in/en/laptops/thinkpad/
11. Green Web Surfing http://www.brighthub.com/environment/green-computing/articles/31157.aspx

12

Library Automation and Library Services in ICT Environment

Veena Dubey
Guest Lecturer, Kamala Nehru College, Korba, C.G.

ABSTRACT

The emergence of information and communication technology has brought the revolution in the libraries and information centres. The existence of ICT does not change the meaning of library but it has changed the way of doing work and handling services to readers in a more effective way. Library services act as a bridge between the user and its resources. Library services are day by day expanding with the involvement of computer and internet facility in libraries. Although its name is also extended as information centres from library. In this chapter, we will discuss the major ICT applications used in the libraries. Firstly we will go through library automation and then to library services in ICT environment.

Keywords : Information and communication technology, Library automation, Library services.

INTRODUCTION

The word "automation" has been derived from Greek word "automose" means something which has the power of spontaneous motion or self-movement. The term "Automation" was first introduced by D.S. Harder in 1936, who was then with General Motor Company in the U.S. He used automation to mean automatic handling of parts between progressive production processes[1]. Library automation means to automate or computerize all those functions of the library which are earlier carried out by the library professionals. These tasks are generally repetitive in nature. These are the routine tasks of the library like– acquisition, cataloguing, serial control, circulation, etc. Library automation is possible only with the help of a computer. Now a day's computers are used in all walks of life. The impact of computers has virtually permitted to all sectors of library/information work. The work of computer in the library has been dominated with the advent of the microcomputer. The computer has brought many changes in the library and information centre. It has influenced the working methods of all library professionals and librarians. It is not only helpful for library professionals, librarians but also very helpful for readers who come to the library to get their required materials. Library automation refers to the use of computers to automate the typical procedures of libraries such as cataloguing and circulation.

Library Automation is a process of using the machinery for easily working and saving the human power and time[2].

International encyclopedia of information technology and library science defines automation is technology concerned with the design and development of the process and system that minimizes the necessity of human intervention in their operation[3].

Swihart, Stanley S. and Hefley, Beryl F. have defined the term library automation as "the processing of certain routine clerical function in the library with the assistance of computer or other mechanized or semi-automatic equipment"[4].

NEEDS FOR LIBRARY AUTOMATION

Progress, up gradation, and development with time is the natural process. Each and every organization modernizes with time, condition and atmosphere. In the same way automation of library with the emergence of the computer, various library automation software, and other information techniques are the time influenced natural phenomena. Everything in the universe is upgrading day by day with time. If there is no up gradation and development then, that organization will not survive for long time and it becomes dead after few years. That's why Dr. Ranganathan has written in 5th law as "library is a growing organism"[5]. To maintain its growth we have to change its handling and other techniques like services, a way of searching documents etc, as the demand of present society. Earlier we used simple mobile phones for talking but now a day everyone is using smart-phones for talking as well using it as minicomputer like using social networking site i.e. Whatsapp, facebook, e-mail, and also surfing internet. So this is due to development in technology and up gradation in our living standards.

There exist various reasons behind the automation of libraries. These reasons are as follows :

Persists the importance of the library in the digital age : In this modern era, our government is focusing on the use of digital resources and also we are celebrating digital India week. So it has become the most essential need of the library to automate the library services because this will be useful for librarian as well as for readers.

To increase the efficiency of working speed of the library : The use of computer speeds up the flow of the work within any organization. New books, reports, and other materials can, therefore, be released sooner without any delay. It may be time taking in starting but later on, it becomes very easy. Library tasks are generally repetitive in nature.

Systematic and accurate archival of records : There

are various types of records occur in the library i.e., bills, order lists, catalogue cards, accession no maintenance, question papers, etc. So to keep all these records inaccurate manner we can easily take the help of computer and arrange them in most useful form.

Data calculation : Computer has a great memory and we can also expand it according to our need. As stated in above point that through automation we can keep Systematic and accurate archival of records. So if you want to calculate any information regarding no of books, books on the particular subject, other information, we can easily get that without any delay.

Budget : Now a day the cost of computers is decreasing and its speed and capacity go on increasing. So, we don't have to think much about the cost of automation. Even though some library software are available free of cost like, e-granthalaya, KOHA, etc. So with the help of these software we can easily automate our library.

Knowledge explosion : There is much information is available on a particular topic. So it is very difficult to handle all the information manually but with the help of automation, we can handle a large amount of data.

AREAS OF LIBRARY AUTOMATION

Library routine works are generally repetitive in nature. So we have to automate all those works which are same in nature. These are acquisition, cataloguing, serial control, circulation, data processing and retrieval. Let us discuss each section on by one.

Acquisition Section

This involves various process like book selection, book ordering, book receiving, invoice, accessioning, gifts taken, budget allocation, etc. There are various methods for selecting the names of the documents required in the library.

- Firstly we have to take a list of the books from the head of departments, faculty members, students, etc.

Secondly we have to collect the name of the essential books from the circulation register. Those books which are frequently used by the reader are important and useful for them. So purchase some additional copies of it. After collecting names from various sources, make a final list for purchasing books.

- The books which are in the final lists, their other information should be recorded from the bibliographic data sources like publisher's catalogue or online databases.
- An order form is filled mentioning the full bibliographic details of the documents. The details may include the name of the author, title, publisher, ISBN, date of publication, edition, etc. Beside there the order form includes the information regarding present cost, number of copies to be processed in the library and the name of the account through which bill can be paid.

Order can be placed by three different ways –

- Directly it is given to publisher.
- It can be given to bookseller.
- It can be given to a vendor, through quotation.

Once the order is placed librarian has to wait for the due date. If books are received within the due date then it's good but if it gets delay then librarian has to send reminders. If any answer regarding reminder is not coming then the order can be cancelled and given to the next bookseller, vendor.

At the time of receiving, we have to verify books from the order list and then start accessioning of the book. After it, bills should be paid through the allocated funds. Sometimes books can be taken in the library as gifts, and these records must be kept in the different registers. Bills are updated regularly and after processing of each bill, library budget should be maintained properly. So, all these functions are carried out by the acquisition section.

Cataloguing

The catalogue is a list carries the holdings of a library. It is a vital link between the reader and the book. It serves as a key to ascertain the availability of books in the library and gives it call number. Thus a library catalogue has got to be order and updated continuously to show the resources hold by the library. The catalogue is not essential, but its value will be increasingly felt with the expansion of the library. It is no exaggeration saying that a library without a proper catalogue is not of any worth to any institution, and schools are no exception. A borrower should be able to locate a book in the catalogue whose, author, title and subject are known.

C.A.Cutter has defined a library catalogue as an efficient instrument intended to achieve the following objectives[6] –

- To enable a person to find a book of which the author, title or subject is known.
- To know what library has by a given author or a given subject or in a given kind of literature.
- To assist in the choice of books as to its edition (bibliography) or as to its character.

In automation process, we do the same thing with the help of computer. We have to follow certain procedure for that and these are as follows;

- Allow cataloguer to enter various data in the various fields, like title, author, publisher, and accession no, pages, costs, call number etc.
- Generally, these fields are based on the MARC 21 fields.
- There is a field for keywords. In this field, we enter keywords for the records, with the help of Sear's list of subject heading.
- In this way, a database is created for all the library records.
- There is also an option for catalogue cards, by AACR-II, when we click on it the catalogue card get

automatically created. We can also take print out of it.

- Once the records are entered, a database is automatically created. These databases are very helpful for searching the documents to the user. There is another module called as OPAC (Online public service catalogue).This module provides us the facility to search the document by various approaches like – author, title, subject, etc.

Serial Control

Serial includes newspapers, journals, annuals, periodicals, etc. Serials are also referred to periodicals. These publications are published at regular intervals in series with a certain frequency. The frequency may be weekly, fortnightly, monthly, quarterly, etc. Serials are the most important collection of any library because it contains recent information in the concerned field in which it belongs.

Modes of acquisition of periodicals include subscription, gifts, and exchange. In case of subscription, the payment of subscription period which is usually annual is made in advance to the publisher or supplier. Hence it needs a special management system. Libraries which subscribes to a large number of periodicals have a separate section dedicated to managing periodical acquisition and services, called a periodical section. This section is generally found in special libraries.

There are various steps for procuring and maintaining it in automation. These are as follows;

- Subscription involves selection of periodicals, send subscription letter to publisher/supplier, keying in serial data and maintaining subscription file.
- Earlier serials which are coming to the library they get checked if necessary then subscribe it for next year, if they are not necessary then cancel its present subscription.

- Accessioning of individual issues, when the issues are received.
- Sending reminders, to publisher /supplier in case of any delay.
- Check-in, routing.
- Preparation of various lists i.e. list of periodicals to be renewed, list of periodicals received/cancelled during a specified period.
- Keep records of amount send on serials, subscription, binding, etc.
- Estimation of the budget.
- Binding of the whole volume at the end of the year and assign a accession no to it.

Hence the system has the ability to perform these operations accurately and it also generates report whenever necessary. It produces various types of reports. It must have the advanced features to handle complicated procedures of binding control. The data pertaining to vendor file must be same as automated acquisition system.

Circulation Section

Circulation section includes various clerical works i.e. issue and returning of books to the reader, generation of library cards, renewal of cards, reissue of books, charging and discharging from readers, etc. There are large numbers of repeated tasks which can be done automatically. These are as follows;

- Automatically generates library cards for users by doing various kinds of entries in the system like – name, class, address, etc.
- Issuing and returning of books to the user through library software.
- Renewal of library cards after the completion of one year.
- System generated procedure for reservation of issued materials.

- Calculation of overdue charges with the help of system.
- Lending and receiving of books through inter-library loan.
- Systematic storage of records by the system and it also generate various types of reports when needed.

In the same way it performs various miscellaneous tasks.

CRITERIA FOR CHOOSING LIBRARY AUTOMATION SOFTWARE

Whenever we are investing a huge amount in any material, then its selection is a somewhat difficult task. Selection is the basic step for purchasing any material. Whenever we have to select books for the library we also do the selection of books. So there are various principles behind selecting it. In the same way, whenever we have to automate our library our library, we have to consider following points in your mind, these are as follows;[7]

General issues

- Acceptability of software
- Cost
- Applicability in the library system
- Reputation of software designer
- Reputation and goodwill of software supplier

Technical issues

- Language of the interfaces
- Operating system
- Requirement of hardware configuration
- Additionally required software for implementing the automation software
- Data storage capacity.
- Easy to use or not.

Support provided by the software developers

- Availability of documentation of the product/software
- Support for software installation by the supplier
- User training facility from the supplier/developer
- Obtainability of further modifications
- Obtainability of new versions in future
- Club/group of existing software users for discussing issues

Legal Issues

- Registration/copyright of the product
- Acceptable provisions of Warranty statement

PROBLEMS IN LIBRARY AUTOMATION

Earlier we have discussed the needs and benefits of library automation, but there are some drawbacks too. So, we shall discuss these, one by one as follows;

Need of skilled staff : All library professionals are not expert in computers. Even though they feel very difficult to work on it. So it is really essential for any organization to select skilled staff so that he can easily handle computer as well as library works.

Library budget : In libraries, library budget is a great challenge that every librarian has to face while procuring any materials for the library. Library automation initially needs a lot of investment on computers, scanner, printer, barcode reader, software, etc. So, every parent organization has to provide some special grants for automation of library, so that it helps librarian to automate the whole library.

Data entry in database : There are four main areas of automation i.e. acquisition, cataloguing, serial control, and circulation. In each area, we have to create database by entering required information in the various fields. So it is very difficult task to complete these entries. It is a very time taking process.

Electricity : Computer requires electricity for its working. So in automation whole library depends upon electricity. If it goes then readers and library staff should have to face difficulty in issuing, returning and doing other library works. So, proper supply of electricity is also required.

SOME LIBRARY AUTOMATION SOFTWARE

SOUL

SOUL stands for Software for University Library. SOUL is integrated library management software (ILMS). It is designed and developed by INFLIBNET (Information and library network). It is developed for college and university libraries. It is user–friendly software developed to work with client–server model. The first version of SOUL was SOUL1.0 and released during CALIBER 2000. The latest version of SOUL is SOUL 2.0 released in January 2009.

SOUL2.0 supports international standards such as MARC 21, Unicode, multilingual bibliographic format, NCIP2.0 and SIP2. SOUL consists of six modules –

- Acquisition
- Cataloguing
- Circulation
- Serial control

- OPAC (Online Public Access Catalogue)
- Administration

KOHA

KOHA is the world's first free and open source, integrated library management software. Open source software means its source code can be modified to get advanced features. It was created in 1999 and was developed in 2000 by Katipo Communication for the Horowhenua library trust in New Zealand. It is web-based integrated library management software. It runs on Windows, Linux, Mac OS, etc. It provides various web2.0 facilities like tagging, comment, social sharing, RSS feeds etc. A large number of languages are available in it. It has powerful searching and an enhanced catalogue display that can use content from Google, Amazon, Library Thing, Open Library, and others. Standard library protocols are used in it i.e. MARC21, Z39.50, SIP2, SIP/NCIP, etc. These standards facilitate its interoperability with other integrated library management software. It's all modules are based on standards used for World Wide Web technologies-XHTML.

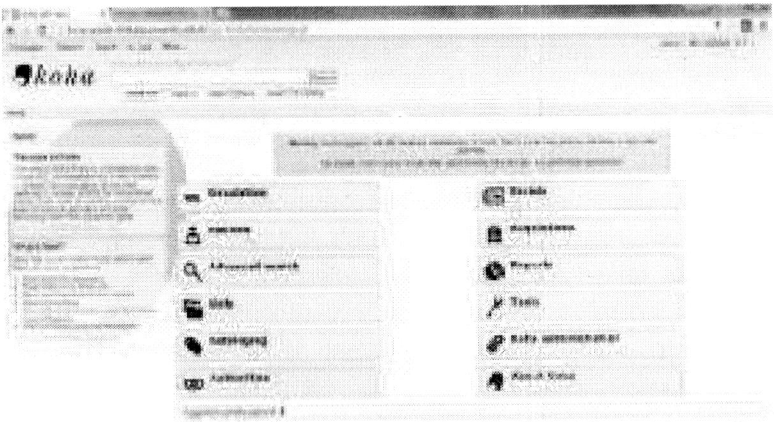

It has eight modules. These are as follows

- OPAC
- Full Catalogue

- Circulation
- Serials
- Acquisition
- Patron Management
- Branch Management
- Reservation

LIBRARY SERVICES IN ICT ENVIRONMENT

Five laws of library science act as a powerful guiding force for development and management of library services. These laws of the library can be fulfilled only by providing library services. Library services are the key elements in the library. Different laws support different types of services. Services act as a bridge between the user and library resources.

The primary function of a library or information centre remains the same, i.e. to acquire, organize, and provide access to information to the user. The ways through which these tasks have been carried out have changed tremendously. Libraries have developed new services as per the needs of highly demanding present generation uses.

Library services mean all the services which are provided in the library for efficient and effective uses of library resources and to satisfy the user demand. Various types of library services are provided in different types of libraries. These are as follows reference services, referral services, current awareness services, literature search services, document delivery services, translation services, selective dissemination of information, indexing and abstracting services, reprographic services, bibliographic services etc. Library services after the emergence of information technology are as – Integrated library management system, online public access catalogue, inter-library loan, audio-visual services, library extension services.

The vast change in form of library services exists with the emergence of web 2.0 technology because web 2.0 is the interactive web. We can easily communicate with others, who are in remote locations. Web 2.0 acts as a boon for library professionals epically for providing various library services. The term web 2.0 was officially coined in 2004 by Dale Dougherty, vice president of O'Reilly Media Inc, during a team discussion on a potential future conference about the web.[6] (*www.netugc.com/web2.0*). When web 2.0 is used for providing the library services then it is known as library 2.0. The term "Library 2.0" was coined by Michael Casey in his blog "Library Crunch".[8](liswiki.org/wiki/library-2.0).

TYPES OF LIBRARY SERVICES

Current Awareness Services

This service is provided to the user for keeping them up to date about the new materials which are procured by the library. These materials are– periodicals, journals, magazines, etc. This service is used in academic and special libraries. Now a day this service is provided in the form of Table of Contents (TOC), alerts, List of new arrivals of journals and books, press clippings, research digest, including abstracting and indexing services.

Selective Dissemination of Information

Selective dissemination of information was the concept first described by Hans Peter Luhn of IBM in 1958. SDI attempts to facilitate user's information retrieval and information filtering needs. It saves the user time and effort. The goal of SDI is to deliver new information available in the library to those users, who express their interest via use profile. There are two major components of SDI – User profile and Document profile. The user profile comprises a set of keywords which are decided and written by the user. Document profile contains the database of all the materials available in the library. The searching mechanism is used for matching keywords between user profile and the document profile. At the end, searched result is shown to the user.

Instant Chatting

This offers simultaneously transmission of text-based messages from sender to receiver. This is used for providing reference services to those users who are in remote places. It is also used among library professionals.

Database Creation

Accession register is the database of the library. But now days we are using various software for creating a database of the library. These are– Oracle RDBMS, IBM DB2, Microsoft SQL Server, SAP Sybase ASE, Microsoft access, My SQL, etc. With the help of these software, we can create the database of our own library. Publishers are using it in great extent for selling their books and other materials. Some important database are – ABI/Inform (Business field), Academic search (Multidisciplinary), Engineering village (engineering, geosciences and physics), JSTOR (Multidisciplinary), PsycINFO (Psychology), etc. Librarian can use it as a tool for procuring various documents in the library in related fields.

Electronic Document Delivery Services

Its name itself clarifies the meaning of this service. It is generally used for scholarly communication. In this service, the required document is supplied to the user either by e-mail, fax or by using other technology. Earlier documents were delivered either by library attendant or by post; etc. It takes more time, cost and effort.

Scanning and Printing Technology

Scanner and printer are the key elements for providing various services. Printer helps to take print out the pages from the computer if necessary. The scanner helps in scanning text, images, and content pages of books.

E-Resources

E-Resources mainly include e-books, and e-journals. Electronic resources are very important for providing library services in the ICT environment. This information is in computer readable form. These follow various standards protocol, DRM (Digital Rights Management), access, archiving, privacy, and other features. These resources can be accessed by various no. of users at a time. It can be accessed 24 hours in a day without any boundation. Some resources are available on the internet and can be accessed easily. Many publishers provide their resources by paying subscription cost. Some of the publishers who are providing e-resources are– emerald, Elsevier, Kluwer, Springer, High wire, John Wiley, etc.

Indexing and Abstracting Services

These services are provided by librarians/publishers for giving the review of the content available in the given article or book. This is very helpful for those who do not have time to go through whole content and selects material by reading abstracts only. But in ICT era publishers are providing it free of cost in the internet and anyone can go through the abstract and contents of the book/journal/article and then only he /she can subscribe it. So it is useful for other users as well as librarian. Now day's abstracts are prepared automatically and known as automated abstracting. The concept of automated indexing was given by Eugene Garfield[9] (http://www.netugc.com/indexing-and-abstracting-service).

Institutional Repositories

Institutional repository is the intellectual output of any organization in the form of articles, journals, books chapters, book, thesis, dissertation, project reports, question papers, etc. Institutional repositories are created by using digital library software i.e. D-Space, Greenstone, e-prints, fedora, etc. It is the best way for online archival, collection, preserving and dissemination of intellectual output of the institution.

N-LIST (National Library and Information Services Infrastructure for Scholarly Content)

NLIST is an initiative of Ministry of Human Resource Development under National Mission on Education through ICT to extend e-resources to colleges in India. This project is executed by UGC-INFONET (INFLIBNET) and INDEST – AICTE Consortium.

CONCLUSION

Library automation is the process which needs proper planning, timely implementation and periodical evaluation. The librarian with the administrators has to set the priorities after analyzing the current status and future requirements. Selection of the suitable integrated library management package according to the needs of the users and the library is important. For the successful implementation of an integrated library system, all key factors must be in place support from administration, staff, competence, consideration of user requirements, the presence of infrastructure, (Hardware, software, networks) available data, excellent managerial skill from the librarian. The ICT also influenced the nature of services delivered by a library.

REFERENCES

1. E-resource: sodhganga.inflibnet.ac.in/bitstream/10603/5661/9/09-chapter%204.Pdf.
2. E-resource: https://en.wikipedia.org/wiki/category:Library_Automation.
3. E-resource: sodhganga.inflibnet.ac.in/bitstream/10603/5661/9/09-chapter%204.Pdf.
4. E-resource: sodhganga.inflibnet.ac.in/bitstream/10603/13526/11/11-chapter%201pdf.
5. S.R.Rangnathan, Five laws of Library science (1931).
6. Krishna Kumar, Theory of cataloguing.
7. Central Board of Secondary Education, Library and Information Science, page no: 144.
8. E-resource: liswiki.org/wiki/library-2.0
9. E-resource: www.netugc.com/indexing and abstracting services.

13

An Introduction to Academic Library Consortia in India

Pankaj Kumar

Librarian, Govt. Shahid Venkat Rao Degree College, Bijapur, C.G.

ABSTRACT

UGC-INFONET is the most motivated project for academic intuitions and it is supported by the University Grants Commission, Government of India. It delivers various types published electronic resources in various academic disciplines for the research community. This consortium is a joint effort of UGC, INFLIBNET and ERNET to interlink all academic universities and colleges of the country and facilitates them with a subscription of scholarly electronic journals. UGC – INFONET digital library consortium is a boon for the academic development. It is not only helping to more than 350 universities and about 14,000 colleges affiliated with these universities and approximately 10 million students to access the e-journals.

Keywords : UGC Infonet, Library consortia, E-resources, Scholarly communication, Acamedic library consortia

INTRODUCTION

It is not possible for one library or information centres to hold the full stock of information resources or to procure all information, which may be in demand by its clientele. .Even not a single library or information centre, can meet the thrust of knowledge of all the readers from its holdings. To solve this problem, library cooperation started long ago, such as interlibrary loan, document delivery, library networks, etc. At present, the more accepted system of resource sharing is called library consortium. A library consortium is a group of two or more libraries that have agreed to cooperate with each other in order to fulfil certain similar needs, usually resource sharing. Cooperation among libraries is not a new concept. It has existed in many forms, in many countries, for many years. Some cooperation was, and still is, informal while other types encompass complex processes to share collections or services. Traditionally, library cooperation meant sharing collections in some way, but it could also include sharing of services, or of processes such as joint cataloguing of materials, or of staff and user training. In general, however, most libraries kept their autonomy and consortia involvement was a peripheral library service. Cooperative efforts usually had an economic motivation, and that incentive continues today. Recent developments in library funding and the growth in importance of electronic materials have led to a change in thinking about how libraries cooperate and the growth of formal cooperative entities.

DEFINITION

Library consortium is a "community (a cooperative) of two or more information agencies which have formally agreed to coordinate, cooperate or consolidate certain function" to achieve mutual objectives. It is an association of a group of libraries to achieve mutually the joint benefits. It provides a way for its members to conduct business in a comparative manner.

NEED OF LIBRARY CONSORTIA

Overloaded budget

Libraries are committing larger portions of their budgetary allocations for either procuring or assessing electronic resources while the allocation keeps on diminishing. The libraries with their diminishing or at best static financial allocations have to consider new ways to consolidate globally accessible electronic resources. Consortia are formed with an objective to enhance the purchasing power of the participating institutes in this critical situation of major financial crunch faced by the libraries and information centre. A consortium facilitates the member libraries to get the benefit of wider access to electronic resources at an affordable cost and at the best terms of licenses.

Information explosion

The voluminous growth of literature has made it impossible for a library to attain self-sufficiency. Library materials have grown exponentially in many forms and formats. Today new materials and electronic versions of old materials is resulting in the availability of information in numerous forms. This shows Information flood. So a consortium is a better position to address and resolve the problems of managing, organizing and archiving the many form and format resources.

Impossibility of self-sufficiency

With the multiplication of information in a great number or heap forms, it is difficult for any library to be fully sufficient to provide a supply of information needs of its user community. Financial limitation, space curb, human resources inadequacy also stress upon the need for the libraries to conclude for the consortia approach

Quick Access

The technology provides a large number of media

devices for delivery of information with greater speed and economy. Academic and Research users now hope to access to rich online resources like article journals e-books in electronic form as the electronic access is comparatively cheaper. Users are beginning to expect an electronic delivery that is speedy and accessible at the remote.

Diversity of user needs

The technology has changed expectations of researchers, their patience, and their will to accept services that are available on demand. The Web-based electronic resources are a suitable answer to the expectations of users. Library users want to have access to that material as quickly as possible, and many of them want information on their computer screens.

BENEFITS OF CONSORTIA

Consortia will give the library and also the user Extended access that is, better service for reduced costs. The advantages of having consortia are as follows:

Reduced Information Cost

Many libraries currently subscribe only to those Journals that they can afford. Though interested in other journals yet they cannot afford to provide access to them. Consortia approach helps them to provide the access.

Document Delivery Service

Inter-libraries loan services will grow and it is interlinked with the search of the union catalogues which will build effective Document Delivery Service (DDS). Delivery of documents will be fast, electronically through Xeroxing, fax, courier or email.

Solve Space Problem

Since the subscribed resources would be accessible online in electronic format, the beneficiary institutions would have less pressure on space requirement for storing and managing print-based library resources. Moreover, all problems associated with print media such as their wear and tear, location, shelving, binding, organizing, etc. would not be an issue for electronic resources.

CONSORTIA MODELS

The types of consortia identified are generally based on various models evolved in India in variety of forms depending upon participations affiliation and funding sources.

Open Consortia

This type of consortia is very flexible and it is the wish of members of consortia can join and leave any they please. INDEST Consortium is an example to this.

Closed grouped Consortia

This type's consortiums have a defined group. This kind of consortia appears either by attachment and association among them likes CSIR, DAE, and IIM Consortium.

Centrally Funded consortia

In this type, the consortium will solely depend on the parent body. A few examples are by UGC- INFONET, ICMR, and DSIR.

Shared-budget consortia

In this model, the participating libraries take the lead and form the consortium. IIM and FORSA are examples of this model.

ACADEMIC LIBRARY CONSORTIUM

UGC INFONET DIGITA'. LIBRARY CONSORTIUM

The UGC INFONET Digital Library Consortium was formally launched in December 2003 by Honourable Dr. A P J Abdul Kalam, the President of India soon after providing the Internet connectivity to the universities in the year 2003 under the UGC Infonet programme. The Consortium proved to be a recipe to university libraries which have been discontinuing subscription of scholarly journals because of "Serials Crisis". The term "serials crisis" refers to exponential and continuing increase in subscription cost of scholarly journals. The crisis is a result of the rise in the cost of journals much faster than the rate of inflation, increase in number of journals and the paucity of funds available to the libraries. The Consortium provides current as well as archival access to more than 7500+ core and peer reviewed journals and 10 bibliographic databases from 26 publishers and aggregators in different disciplines. The programme has been implemented in phased manner. In the first phase that began in 2004, access to e-resources was provided to50 universities who had Internet connectivity under the UGC Infonet Connectivity programme of the UGC. In the second phase, 50 more universities were added to the programme in the year 2005. So far 209 Universities including 14 National Law schools and central universities that come under the purview of UGC have been provided differential access to subscribed e-resources. These e-resources covers almost all subject disciplines including arts, humanities, social sciences, physical sciences, chemical sciences, life sciences, computer sciences, mathematics and statistics, etc. The programme is wholly funded by the UGC and executed by the INFLIBNET (Information and Library Network) Centre, Gandhinagar.

Aims and Objectives

The main objective of the UGC INFONET Digital Library Consortium is to provide access to qualitative electronic resources including full-text and bibliographic databases to academic institutions at a lower rate of subscription. The major aims and objectives of the UGC-Infonet Digital Library Consortium are as follows;

- To provide access to high-quality and scholarly electronic resources to a large Number of academic institutions including universities and colleges at substantially lower rates of subscription and at most favourable terms and conditions.

- To promote rapid and efficient access to scholarly content to the users and to create and promote the use of ICT in teaching and learning in universities in India.
- To impart training to the users, librarians, research scholars and faculty members of the institutions in use of electronic resources with an aim to optimize their usage and promote maximum use of e-resources.
- To promote interaction and inter-library cooperation amongst the participating Universities.

Benefits

Major benefits of UGC-INFONET Digital Library Consortium are as follows :

- It improves the present library services and decreases the payment cost
- The Consortium acts as a single-window service for a large number of universities with their various research and academic interest
- UGC-INFONET Digital Library Consortium provides international databases and full-text resources; which improves research productivity of institutions.
- The Consortium is offered better terms of agreement for use, archival access and preservation of subscribed electronic resources.
- All problems related to print media such as their wear and tear, location, shelving, binding, organizing, etc. are not an issue for electronic resources. Because UGC-INFONET Digital Library Consortium by accessing resources is available online in e- formats.

Electronic Resources

Ugc–infonet digital library consortium provides the following full-text electronic journals and bibliographic databases to its academic network for their research and development.

FULL TEXT E-RESOURCES

- American Chemical Society: www.pubs.acs.org/
- American Institute of Physics:
- American Physical Society.
- Annual Reviews: http://arjournals.annualreviews.org/
- Wiley-Blackwell Publishing: www3.interscience.wiley.com/
- Cambridge University Press: http://journals.cambridge.org/
- Elsevier Science: www.sciencedirect.com/
- Emerald: www.emeraldinsight.com
- Institute of Physics: www.iop.org/EJ/
- J-STOR: www.jstor.org/
- Nature: www.nature.com/
- Oxford University Press: www.oxfordjournals.org
- Portland Press: www.portlandpress.com/pp/journals/default.htm
- Project Euclid: http://projecteuclid.org/
- Project Muse: http://muse.jhu.edu/
- Royal Society of Chemistry: www.rsc.org/Publishing/Journals/
- SIAM: http://epubs.siam.org/
- Springer Link: www.springerlink.com/
- Taylor and Francis.

Bibliographic databases

- SciFinder Scholar
- MathSciNet: www.ams.org/mathscinet/
- Royal Society of Chemistry (6 Databases): www.rsc.org/Publishing/

- Current Awarenr ss/index.asp
- ISID: http://isid.org.in/
- JCCC

Open access resources

- Open Access E-Journals.
- Open Access Directories.
- IRs@member Institutions:

COLLEGE MODEL OF THE CONSORTIUM

The INFLIBNET Centre is also working closely with MHRD to extend e –resources to all its affiliated colleges under the National Mission on Education through ICT. The proposal named "National Library and Information Services Infrastructure for Scholarly Content" (N-LIST) is being evolved in collaboration with the UGC-INFONET Digital Library Consortium and the INDEST-AICTE Consortium, IIT Delhi.

CONCLUSION

UGC-Infonet Digital Library Consortium is the most important consortium for teaching and research activities and providing to a large array of e-resources to all academic universities and colleges in India and thus facilitates the quick access and efficient and effective usage of e-resources for teaching and research activities.

REFERENCES

1. Bansodek, S. Y. (2007). LIBRARY CONSORTIA IN INDIA: ISSUES AND PROSPECTS. V3 (2)(July-December).
2. Bhatt, R. (2010). Use of UGC-Infonet Digital Library Consortium resources by research scholars and. library management, vol.31.
3. BOSTICK, S. L. (n.d.). Academic Library Consortia in the United States:. LIBER QUARTERLY.
4. Hiremath, U. (2001). "Electronic consortia: resource sharing in the digital age. emerald.

5. KAUR, S. V. (n.d.). Implications of Library Consortia: How the Indian Libraries are benefited.
6. Ramesh Yernagula, &. P. (n.d.). Library Consortia: benefits and models of E-journals Consortia. kanpur.
7. Shalu Bedi. (n.d.). Library Consortia: A Step forward the Information Society. chandigarh: punjab university.
8. www.ugc-infonet consortium

14

Use of Barcode Technology in the Library

Abhishek Singh Rajput
Professional Assistant, Sri Venkatwasra College (University of Delhi), Delhi

ABSTRACT

This article covers various aspects and components of barcode technology in automated and computerized libraries. Barcode is a set of black and white line. The black and white line is formed by the same barcode and one reader is needed to read this. The barcode technology used in the automated and computerized library for providing quick services to the users. Barcode technology works on a principle which is called symbology. Symbology in its basic form is what defines the barcode; it determines the mapping and interpretation of the encoded information or data. Some barcode technology systems use two separate widths to determine the character while others use multiple width lines. The use of any of these encoding styles depends, of course, on the application for which the barcode technology is being used.

Keywords : Barcode, Barcode Symbology, Barcode scanner

INTRODUCTION

A barcode is the small image of lines (bars) and spaces that is affixed to retail store items, identification cards, and postal mail to identify a particular product number, person, or location. The code uses a sequence of vertical bars and spaces to represent numbers and other symbols[5]. A bar code symbol typically consists of five parts: a quiet zone, a start character, data characters (including an optional check character), a stop character, and another quiet zone[1]. In an automated system, using barcode technology, the member surrenders his/her identity card and the counter staff can scan it. It is a group of thick and thin lines that is placed on a product so that a computer can get the price of the product and other information about it. Barcode is a set of black and white line black and white line is formed by the same barcode. A barcode reader is needed to read this. Now-a-days many libraries are the using barcode to provide services. It saves the time of the user and proving effective.

DEFINITION OF BARCODE

"A code consisting of a group of printed and variously patterned bars and spaces and sometimes numerals that are designed to be scanned and read into computer memory and that contains information (as identification) about the object it labels[2]."

ABOUT THE BARCODE

The first barcode system or barcode technology was developed around the time of the 1940s and 1950s, since then people have become very accustomed to their use, through common applications such as in retail and grocery markets. Their first working system used ultraviolet ink, but the ink faded too easily and was rather expensive[7].

ADVANTAGES OF BARCODE

There are many advantages of the barcode system. They are as follows;

- Accuracy of data input (error free)
- Benefit from Customer or Regulatory Requirements
- It Cuts Costs
- Improve & Developed Operational Efficiency
- Labour saving by avoiding manual system
- Measurement of work in progress throughout the factory
- More accurate dispatch cost efficient
- Rapid access to total production costs
- Real-time data collection
- Reduce Errors in data input
- Represent unique identity of a particular product
- Time-saving
- Energy saving
- Ease of Implementation

DISADVANTAGES OF BARCODE

There are many disadvantages of the barcode system. They are discussed as follows;

- System Failure may cost more delays.[8]
- Scratched or crumpled barcodes may cause problems
- Data must be coded in the barcode
- In laser scanning, durability and cost are the two disadvantages[8].

REQUIREMENTS FOR BARCODE APPLICATION

Implementing barcodes in library applications using for library automation technology, following hardware and software are required:

- Barcode Scanner

- Communication Software
- Database of Library Holdings
- Decoder
- Inventory Control
- Library Software (like Libsys, KOHA, SOUL)
- Membership Database
- Personal Computers
- Printer
- Printing Software

BARCODE SYMBOLOGY

The barcode Symbologies are systems for encoding data/information such that a scanner or a decoding system may together read and decode the data/information encoded in the barcode. The actual technique of encoding the bars and spaces a number of technical specifications or characteristics define and separate symbology from another symbology. In the barcode symbologies mapping between messages and barcodes is called a symbology. The specification of a barcode symbology includes the encoding of the single digits (likes 0-9)/characters (likes A-Z) of the message as well as the start and stop markers into bar and space.

TYPES OF BARCODE SYMBOLOGY

A Barcode Symbology defines the technical details of a particular type of barcode: the width of the bars, character set, method of encoding, checksum specifications, etc. Most users are more interested in the general capabilities of a particular symbology (how much and what kind of data can it hold, what are its common uses, etc) than in the excruciating technical details[3]. There are many types of barcodes available. Several barcode Symbology types are available in the market today.

Numeric-only barcodes : This barcode system means Numeric-only barcodes are generally used for retail applications, but there are also used in blood banks, some older libraries and new Libraries. Different numeric barcodes system offer error correction and self-checking features.there are some example is following.

Codabar **:** This code is older code often used in library systems, sometimes in blood banks product code Codabar. This barcode representing characters of 0-9, letters A to D and the following symbols: - $ / + are used.

1234

EAN-13(European Article Numbering System-13): This code is European Article Numbering international retail product code-13. There are consist of 13 Number and is the superset of UPCA. this is the ISBN standards in human readable and non-human readable formats.

1 234567 890128

Alpha-numeric barcodes : Alpha-numeric barcodes are widely used in the healthcare industry because can include a large quantity of information and error reduction. There are some examples as following.

Code 93 **:** This code Compact code similar to Code 39. This barcode representing characters 0-9, A-Z, the space character and the following symbols: /, + ,%, - , . , $.

12AB

LOGMARS (Logistics Applications of Automated Marking and Reading Symbols) **:** This code Same as Code 39, this is the U.S. Government specification. This code defines acceptable ranges for a number of variables, including density, ratio, bar height, and size of the human-readable interpretation line.

Two-Dimensional barcodes : Two-dimensional barcodes are ideal for encoding large amounts of information. The United Parcel Services uses a two-dimensional barcode, Maxicode, in its automated package sorting system. There are some examples as following.

Maxicode : This code fixed length, used by United Parcel Service for automated package sorting. This is a two-dimensional matrix barcode symbology containing hexagon modules in a 1" square area.

QR Code : This code used for material control and order confirmation. QR Code and Barcode both are equally important for the different purposes with respect to the nature of work. In the order of chronology adaptability, the barcode is leading to QR Code. QR Code can encode up to 2509 numeric or 1520 alphanumeric characters and offers three levels of error detection.

Industry Standards for Barcodes and Labels : Different industries have come up with their own barcode systems, creating an industry-universal barcode system. For instance, the Bookland EAN encodes books' ISBN information, for international bookmarking, while the ISSN/SISAC Barcode is used by the Optical Industry Association, for labelling retail optical products. there are some examples as following.

Bookland EAN : This encoded number starts with 978 and known as ISBN Barcode. Bookland EAN is used exclusively with books.

UCC/EAN-128 : This code is used to provide a worldwide format and standard for exchanging common data between companies. This code is done by using application identifiers.

STRUCTURE OF BARCODE

Barcode is a set of black and white line black and white line is formed by the same barcode. and one reader is needed to read this. The barcode reader is referred to by the reader of these lines is needed.A typical barcode consists of the following:

Quiet Zone : The minimum required space for barcode scan-ability, preceding the Start Character of a bar code symbol. The quiet zone should be free from any printing and be the same colour and reflectance as the background of bar code symbol. The Quiet Zone should be ten times the width of the narrowest element in the barcode, or 0.25 inch minimum. This is also known as Clear Area.

Start Code : This indicates the start of the barcode. These are sspecial bar code characters and they signify the start of data to the scanner/reader. Start characters are usually stripped-off and not transmitted to the host.

Data : The actual data the barcode stores.

Check Digit : Check digit (not always present) is a mathematical sum that is used to verify the accuracy of the other elements of the barcode. It is the extra digit added at the end of a bar code to allow the scanner to confirm that it read the bar code correctly. It is typically stripped from the data and not transmitted to the host.

Stop Code : Indicates the stopping point of the barcode. These characters signify the end of data to the scanner/reader. They are also stripped-off and not transmitted to the host.

Trailing Quiet Zone : Another clear space with no printing following the Stop Character.

HOW DOES A BARCODE SCANNER WORK?

Barcode scanners have to be able to read the black-and-white zebra lines on products extremely quickly and feed that information to a computer or checkout terminal, which can identify them immediately using a product database. Here is how they do it.

For the sake of this simple example, let's assume that Barcodes are simple on-off, binary patterns with each black line corresponding to a one and each white line a zero. (We've already seen that real Barcodes are more sophisticated than this, but let's keep things simple.)

- Scanning head shines LED or laser light onto Barcode.
- Light reflects back off barcode into a light-detecting electronic component called a photoelectric cell. White areas of the barcode reflect most light; black areas reflect least.9
- As the scanner moves past the Barcode, the cell generates a pattern of on-off pulses that correspond to the black and white stripes. So for the code shown

here ("black black black white black white black black"), the cell would be "off off off on off on off off."

- An electronic circuit attached to the scanner converts these on-off pulses into binary digits (zeros and ones).
- The binary digits are sent to a computer attached to the scanner, which detects the code as 11101011.

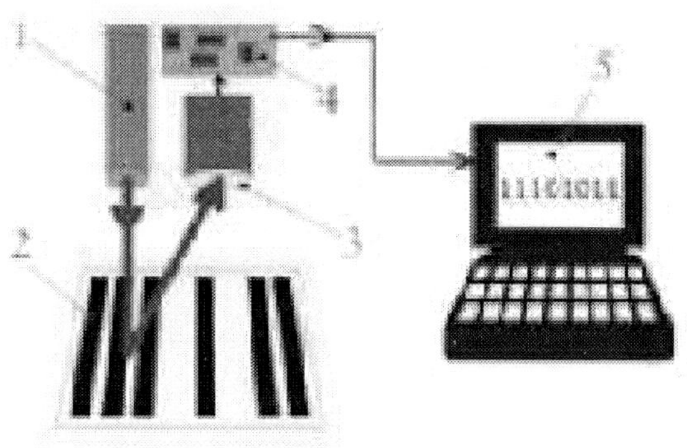

In some scanners, there is a single photoelectric cell and, as you move the scanner head past the product (or the product past the scanner head), the cell detects each part of the black-white barcode in turn. In more sophisticated scanners, there is a whole line of photoelectric cells and the entire code is detected in one go.

In reality, scanners don't detect zeros and ones and produce binary numbers as their output: they detect sequences of black and white stripes, as we've shown here, but convert them directly into decimal numbers, giving a decimal number as their output.

BARCODE READERS

A Barcode Reader is an electronic device that can decode and translate printed Barcodes to a human-readable format on the scanner's screen or on a computer. Barcode Reader typically consist of a light source, a lens and a light sensor that decodes the printed symbol patterns by way of differentiating between dark ink and light background.

Types of Barcode Readers

2D Camera : Some barcodes do not consist of white and black bars, but white and black spaces in a two-dimensional (2D) target. These 2D barcodes cannot be read by standard machinery, but they do allow for versatility of information coding as they can hold and provide much more data than a standard barcode. To read these barcodes, a 2D camera image scanner is necessary. This camera consists of hundreds of tiny lights like the CCD scanner, but these are arranged in multiple rows[12]. The lights flash onto the barcode and take a digital picture of the barcode, which is then sent to software as a digital signal. The software then decodes the information.

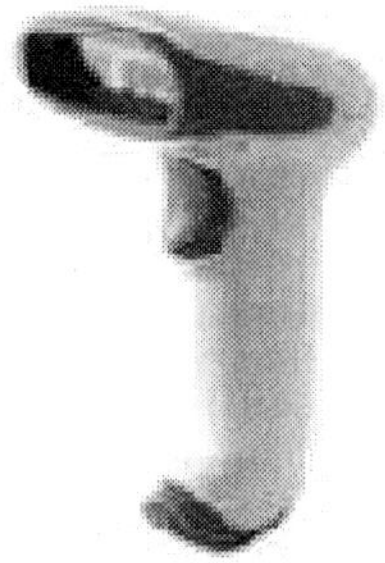

CCD : A charge coupled device (CCD), also known as an LED scanner, features hundreds of tiny LED lights arranged in one long row. These lights are shot directly onto a barcode, and a sensor then measures not the reflection, but the voltage of the ambient light directly in front of each lightbulb. This voltage measurement provides a digital snapshot of the barcode. CCD units can be very expensive, but are highly accurate and versatile pieces of equipment.

Laser : Slightly more advanced than a pen scanner, a

laser barcode scanner is capable of more exact light readings which prevent false positives or scanner errors. In a laser scanner, a laser beam is shot at a mirror inside the actual unit. This mirror makes a movement so that the laser sweeps across the barcode in a straight line[11]. This light then reflects back to a diode, which measures the level of reflection. This reflection is translated into digital signal readout of the barcode. Laser scanners can either be mounted in a scanning unit or be part of a handheld unit.

Pen : Pen barcode readers resemble small wand-type sticks that resemble a small pen. The pen-style barcode reader consists of an LED light and a photodiode in its tip. The user passes this tip over a barcode and the LED light illuminates the black and white bars. The photodiode measures the reflection of light and is able to determine width and colour (white or black) of each bar. This information allows for a digital reading of the barcode, and the information is transmitted to another unit for processing[10].

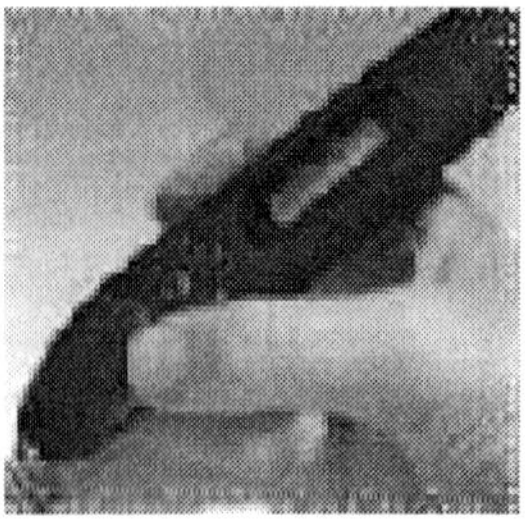

CONCLUSION

The utility of barcoding for automated library transactions is time-tested, and more automated/ computerized libraries in our country are developed/ implement and using this technology. Nearly every Library in automated/computerized Library is using barcode technology to replace keyboard data entry because barcoding is much faster and more accurate than keyboard data entry. The Barcoding technology is a computer aided process of generating codified information (like barcode), which is subsequently printed on a predefined stationary, invariably on a self-adhesive label for several later applications. Every new automated /old automated (implementation of automation) library needs the application of new technology to develop its existing methods. This time thus saved can be utilized for developing advanced and additional techniques in the library.

REFERENCE

1. http://searchmanufacturingerp.techtarget.com/definition/bar-codeRetrieved from (March 18, 2016)
2. http://www.merriam-webster.com/dictionary/bar%20code Retrieved from (Jun 19, 2016)
3. http://www.makebarcode.com/specs/speclist.html Retrieved from (Jun 1, 2016)
4. https://www.barcodesinc.com/articles/barcode-technology.htm Retrieved from (Jun 1, 2016)
5. http://searchmanufacturingerp.techtarget.com/definition/bar-code Retrieved from (Jun 1, 2016)
6. https://www.barcodesinc.com/articles/barcode-technology.htm Retrieved from (Jun 1, 2016)
7. https://en.wikipedia.org/wiki/Barcode Retrieved from (Jun 1, 2016)
8. http://www.slideshare.net/muhammadirtiza9/scanners-barcode-readers Retrieved from (July 10, 2016)
9. http://www.explainthatstuff.com/barcodescanners.html Retrieved from May 7, 2016)

10. http://www.thomasnet.com/articles/automation-electronics/barcode-scanner-types Retrieved from (Jun 15, 2016)

11. http://www.thomasnet.com/articles/automation-electronics/barcode-scanner-types Retrieved from (Jun 15, 2016)

12. Rajput, Abhishek singh (2016). Current Trends in Library Management Systems. International Journal ofInnovative Knowledge Concepts.v2 (08), 09-13p.

13. Rajput, Abhishek Singh (2016). E-Books : A changing scenario from print to electronic metrial. *Vidyawarta*, 01(15), pp.059-061

14. http://www.thomasnet.com/articles/automation-electronics/barcode-scanner-types Retrieved from (Jun 15, 2016)

15

Security System for Libraries: An Introduction to RFID

Manish Kumar Yadav

Librarian, Shyama Prasad Mukherjee Government Degree College, Allahabad, U.P.

ABSTRACT

The purpose of this paper is to provide an overview of radio frequency identification (RFID) systems in libraries. In this paper, the components and technical features of a modern RFID library system are described to provide a guideline for the evaluation of different systems. This paper also discusses the security concerns in RFID technology. This paper describes the usability of RFID technology for the stock verification of library because manual stock verification takes lots of time and labour. But with the advent of RFID technology stock verification can be done in less time as compared to manual stock verification and it also gives accurate result too. The main aim of this paper is to give the detailed information to library professionals about RFID technology and library management software which supports RFID technology so that they can implement it in their libraries and make their library smart.

Keywords : Readers, Technology, antennae, Security systems, library security system

INTRODUCTION

Radio frequency identification (RFID) systems were developed about 30 years ago and were originally niche products. They were used for "radio tracking" of wild and agricultural animals, and evolved later into a technology which is used in many industrial applications today (Kern, 1999).

Librarians have a long history in protecting the privacy of their readers, the library patron. As technology has ushered in more methodologies for the invasion of privacy through electronic means, librarians have become increasingly concerned. The escalating use of radio frequency identification (RFID) tags concerns many people because they open opportunities for inconspicuous scanning of any items a person has with these tags, including their library books. RFIDs are small adhesive-backed tags that transmit a radio signal that easily can be read by a receiver or reader. These tags can be attached to books found in a library or bookstore. While some librarians and the vendors of RFID products for libraries remain convinced that they are secure, the evidence shows that RFIDs create numerous opportunities for privacy invasions. For this reason, librarians must take additional measures to protect patron privacy (Scott Muir, 2007).

TECHNOLOGICAL BACKGROUND

For more than 30 years radio frequency has been used for tracking and in theft detection. This process is very similar to the rather large theft detection clip-on tags used today in many clothing stores, and in other places, except the stores remove those tags. Libraries also made use of this security technology, originally as thin wires hidden in the books that would trigger an alarm if a patron tried to remove the books prior to checkout. The technology worked on the bypass principle in which the trigger in the book was always on, with the staff taking the books from the patron and returning them once the patron was on the exit side of the security gate. These security systems have evolved into the RFID technology with its fuller integration into some library systems of today.

Library RFID technology uses radio waves operating at 13.56 MHz to automatically identifies individual items, such as each individual book. Specific information about that book is stored on a microchip that is attached to a coiled antenna. Often these tags are made from a special silver ink printed on paper or they can be etched. The chip and the antenna together become what is called an RFID tag. RFID tags can be either active– having their own battery power source, or passive – having no power source of its own. Currently, libraries only make use of passive tags, in part due to lower costs, size, and the inability to replace those tags over the lifetime of the battery (Scott Muir, 2007).

Since a *passive* RFID does not have its own power source, it draws power from the reader's magnetic field and uses it to power the microchip's circuits and antenna, which in turn enables the chip to transmit the identification information to the reader. The tag can be placed on the book to reduce wear and the read time for a tag is typically less than 100 milliseconds. Additionally, multiple books with the corresponding tags can be read at once rather than one at a time (Scire, 2003)

COMPONENT INVOLVED IN RFID TECHNOLOGY

RFID Tags

The tag can be paper thin or thick and flexible which allows it to be placed inconspicuously on the inside cover of each book in a library's collection and user's library card. It consists of an etched antenna and a tiny chip, which stores vital bibliographic data including a unique ID number to identify each item. This contrasts with a barcode label, which does not store any information, but merely points to a database. RFID tags can be either active– having their own battery power source, or passive– having no power source of its own. Currently, libraries only make use of passive tags, in part due to lower costs, size, and the inability to replace those tags over the lifetime of the battery (Strickland and Hunt, 2005).

Fig. 1. Image of the tag

RFID reader

RFID readers consist of a transmitter, receiver, antennae and a decoder. They communicate with RFID tags, identify them and retrieve data stored on the tag. Readers can read documents from 30 to 45 cm. The reader is flat like a slate and it is necessary for it to be fixed to a desktop computer and configured with the library software. Since a passive RFID does not have its own power source, it draws power from the reader's magnetic field and uses it to power the microchip's circuits and antenna, which in turn enables the chip to transmit the identification information to the reader. The tag can be placed inside the book to reduce wear and tear. The read time for a tag is typically 100 ms. Additionally, multiple books with corresponding tags can be read at once rather than one at a time (Scire, 2003).

Antennae

The RFID antenna connected to the RFID reader can vary in size and structure, depending on the communication distance required for a given system performance. The antenna activates the RFID tag and transfers data by emitting wireless pulses. Antennae are of two types:

- long-range reader; and
- medium-range reader.

RFID hand reader

The function of an RFID hand reader is the same as that of a flat reader but it is handy and can move around the stacks. It can be connected and configured with a palmtop computer. It needs software to run the program from the palmtop with a wireless connection.

ADVANTAGES OF RFID TECHNOLOGY IN LIBRARY

- It saves time at the circulation counter.
- Theft detection is easy with RFID technology.
- It is easy to trace missing books in the library using RFID hand reader.
- Shelving of books is easy with the help of RFID technology.
- RFID made easy to do the stock verification.

DISADVANTAGES OF RFID TECHNOLOGY IN LIBRARY

- The major disadvantage of RFID technology is its cost.
- Lack of standard.
- Lack of RFID compatible software in India.
- Lack of skilled RFID workers.
- Data security.

LIST OF SOME RFID ENABLED LIBRARY OF INDIA

- Jaykar Library (Pune University), Pune
- SRM University Library, Ghaziabad
- Central Institute of Technology, Kokrajhar Assam
- Lovely Professional University, Punjab etc.

RFID TECHNOLOGY ENABLED LIBRARY MANAGEMENT SOFTWARE

- Koha

- LibSys
- SLIM
- e- Granthalaya 4.0

CONCLUSION

RFID technology has provided major benefits for Library. Because of the growth in its collections the functions like stock verification and tracking of missing books was becoming almost impossible for the library. RFID technology has enabled the library to provide a quick, accurate and timely service to the users. Quick circulation of books means no queuing in front of the circulation counter, and tracking and shelving of the books have become much easier. The manpower required to perform all these functions is now being reduced and is being utilized for providing some extra services. Most importantly the system has already put a check on the theft and misuse of documents, as users understand that the system is in place and capable of detecting theft. The RFID technology has been a boon for the library, as it requires less manpower to service more books and users.

REFERENCES

1. Kern, C. (1999), "RFID-technology; recent development and future requirements", Proceedings of the European Conference on Circuit Theory and Design ECCTD99, Stresa, 30 August-2 September, Vol. 1, pp. 25-8.
2. Scott Muir, (2007),"RFID security concerns", Library Hi Tech, Vol. 25 Iss 1 pp. 95 – 107
3. Scire, T. (2003), "What's next for the radio frequency library?", Library and Archival Security, Vol. 18 No. 2, pp. 51-8.
4. Strickland, L. and Hunt, L. (2005), "Technology, security, and individual privacy: new tools, new threats, and new public perceptions", Journal of the American Society for Information Science and Technology, Vol. 56 No. 3, pp. 221-34
5. Tagsys (2008), "RFID tags", available at: www.tagsysrfid.com/systems/flexible-hf-tags.cfm

16

MOOCs and their Impact on Library & Information Centers: Issues and Challenges

Brundaban Nahak
Librarian
Radhakrishna Institute of Tech. & Engineering
Bhubaneswar, Odisha

ABSTRACT

The main aim of MOOC is to provide opportunities to a large number of learners to attend free online courses from anywhere all over the world. MOOCs have drastically changed the way of teaching and learning procedure. It is a revolutionizing in the field of higher education by giving a new learning opportunity for aspiring students, faculty and universities in many subject areas including Library & Information Science (LIS). Since MOOCs is the latest venture in the education sector, how Library Science Massive Open Online Course (LISc MOOC) can help our professional to deal with Massive Open Learning (MOL). The author mainly gives a brief idea about the concept, history of MOOCs, objective, types, literature review, impact, MOOCs as a professional Development Tool for Librarians, MOOCs in LIS, initiatives taken by Indian Government & Institutions for MOOCs, etc. It is an attempt to touch base with all the areas relating to the impact of MOOCs and Library and Information Centers (LICs) in simple language.

Keywords : Udacity, Coursera, massive open online course (MOOC), connectivist massive open online course (cMOOC).

INTRODUCTION

Technological Developments have brought in tremendous changes in a way the higher education delivered, communicated and also library and information science over a period of time. MOOCs are a new innovation in the field of online learning at massive level and become very much popular in a short period of time in all kinds of disciplines. MOOCs stand for Massive Open Online Courses originally evolved in the year 2008 but enough attention perceived in the academic arena in the year 2012 in which "New York Times" has also declared 2012 year as the year of the MOOC and some key players of MOOCs established benchmarks and standards in MOOCs environments in a short period of time in every discipline. MOOCs can be defined as an online learning model in which anyone who has computer and internet connection can participate virtually in any course without the prerequisites of the traditional education system. Therefore, library and information science professionals started writing research papers, organizing conferences and workshops on MOOCs and LIS issues, creating courses on different topics related to library and information science arena on MOOC.

MEANING OF MOOCS

MOOCs offer online courses with the help of the Internet. Anyone can join from anywhere for any course. Most of the reputed Universities are joining with this noble venture. The internet is the most basic thing to join for online courses. They cut the cost of university education with the quality education. In response to this event, Dave Cormier (University of Prince Edward Island) and Bryan Alexander

(National Institute for Technology in Liberal Education) coined the term "MOOC" or Massive Open Online Course (McAuley et al. 2010). In principle, a MOOC is denoted as:

Massive : as registration is not capped (with enrolment in some cases exceeding 100,000 students);

Open : to take advantage of widely available OER and open registration (though some MOOCs have pre-requisites, and for-fee registrations, examinations or certificates of completion);

Online : with no requirement for face-to-face attendance; and

Course : the concept of a pedagogically designed learning journey.

HISTORICAL DEVELOPMENT OF MOOCS

The term "MOOC" (Massive Open Online Course) was coined by David Cormier in 2008 (Cormier & Siemens, 2010) to describe a twelve-week online course, Connectivism and Connected Knowledge, designed by George Siemens and Stephen Downes and offered at the University of Manitoba, Canada, in Fall semester 2008. Thrun launched Udacity in 2012, a for-profit company providing alternative lifelong learning options primarily in computer science and math. In May 2012, Harvard and MIT launched the non-profit, edX, with the University of California at Berkeley joining soon after. Coursera partners with leading universities to provide educational access to all in 2012.

OBJECTIVES OF THE PAPER

The paper is designed to fulfil the following objectives:

- To identify the difficulties being faced by this Profession & to know the Indian MOOCs
- To find out to what extend LISc MOOC shall be the solution to overcome the difficulties
- To discover the literature published on MOOCs and general issues

TYPES OF MOOCS

MOOCs are broadly classified into C-MOOCs and X-MOOCs.

C-MOOCs : It is a creation for emphasizing connecting learners called as connectivist MOOC and build upon the idea and platform originally visualized by George Siemens.

X-MOOCs : They have their background in the evolution of open courseware and open educational resources. It generally offered by universities in collaboration with a commercial organization/company whose aim is to gain profit & associated mostly with the three largest platform provider's edX, Udacity, and Coursera.

KEY PLAYERS OFFERING MOOCS

The key players of MOOCs are Udacity, Coursera, Edx. The term MOOCs gained momentum in fall of 2011, when Standford University offered three of its engineering courses viz. Artificial Intelligence, Machine learning and Introduction to databases for free on the Internet. This resulted in massive enrollment, which surpassed the imagination of developers of these courses.

Udacity (http://www.udacity.com) was born in 2012 owing to the efforts of the S. Thurn, D. Stevens and M. Sokolsky by raising funds through venture capital. It follows a policy of developing its courses in-house, working with education specialist to make the pedagogy as effective as possible.

Coursera (http://www.coursera) was a biggest among all initiatives established by Daphne Koller and Andrew Ng. It is a profitable company by raising funds through venture capital in 2012. It has partnered with elite universities on revenue sharing model to provide content while it offers hosting and software platform. It has 108 universities and institutes from USA, Europe and Asia-Specific offering different courses.

Edx (http://www.edx.org) was initiated in 2011 by A.

Agrawal with MITx and Harvard University. At present, its consortium consists of 32 top universities from USA, Europe and Asia offering 126 courses. IIT Bombay from India has few recently signed up with Edx to offer of its courses.

CLASSIFICATION OF MOOC COURSES

Moocs can be classified as following categories;

- **Based on course :** Paid & Free
- **Based on pace :** Schedule driven & self-paced
- **Based on course instructors :** University courses & Private firms

LITERATURE REVIEW

A number of studies had already been done worldwide during last few years on MOOCs and a few selective literature reviews will focus on MOOCs in library science.

Bond and Leibowitz (2013) highlighted the MOOC issues with respect to librarians' participation, opportunities and challenges faced because of clubbing serials to the users in MOOC mode.

Creed-Dikeogu and Clark (2013) conducted a literature on MOOCs and academic libraries and discussed the brief history, structure and potential areas in which librarians can participate in order to gear up the MOOC movement through libraries.

Frederiksen (2013) provided a brief description of selected scholarly articles published on MOOCs and LIS professional issues.

Okamoto (2013) is discussed the development, support of, and advocacy for open textbooks by academic libraries, who writes "historically an advocate for access to information and a key campus player in student learning.

WHY MOOC FOR OUR LIBRARY PROFESSION?

The ICT Technology has brought a plethora of improvement in the human dimension, so definitely, we, the

Librarians/Information Officers can also link and improves our status and career by having a MOOC for our profession. The uniqueness of ot r occupational course is that every subject gets imbibed in our course, so why not LIS MOOC. The development and strengthening of Librarianship and LICs at Rural, District or State Level can be made to interconnect using LIS MOOC. The below table shows what are the areas where LIS MOOC can help.

Table 1. LIS MOOC Utility

Reasons	*Utility of MOOC*
Lack of Unified Syllabus	No syllabus is same be it respect to Librarianship or any other discipline so if MOOC courses are developed for the Librarianship the lapse can be followed up.
Limited Refresher Course	A few limited refresher courses are being sponsored by the university for librarianship in every year on the limited seat, MOOC can be the convenient refresher course for any librarianship who wants to join refresher course as per his/ her convenience.
New Development	MOOC can help our profession in knowing the latest concepts and how these concepts can be used for developing improved library services.
Single Cadre/handed	The institute where there is single cadre / handle they are denied the chance to go for any refresher course or attend any courses for their development on account of being single staff, MOOC do come as a blessing.
Inhabitant to use IT	There is generally a trend among the elders of this profession to use IT as they feel very complicated and generally do feel shy to join any short-term courses on the computer. In this regard, MOOC can be helpful in removing this sluggishness to use the IT.

IMPACT OF MOOCS IN ACADEMIC LIBRARIES AND INFORMATION CENTRES

The appeal of MOOCs is a global one, with no time boundaries, as there are perpetual or repeated cycle presentations. No age, nationality, educational, or professional prerequisites exist, although certain MOOCs state that a pre-entry level knowledge is beneficial. This is often not mandatory and certification or proctored examinations are often optional for-fee activities. Major of the students needs to be internet acquainted. Due to the higher cost of traditional education, MOOCs are in practice. It is observed that middle-class families are keen on adopting learning through MOOCs.

- MOOC material can be used multiple times & educational material can share.
- Courses can be shared among institutions & traditional education can be replaced.
- Time-saving, Reduction of equipment & Student support services will be limited

MOOCS AS A PROFESSIONAL DEVELOPMENT TOOL FOR LIBRARIANS

Librarians have for gaining hands-on experience with particular technologies that can help improve their reference and instructional services delivery. There is a broad range of course offering in areas of computer science (specifically, learning new coding languages) for librarians with an interest in developing technological expertise. Courses like (New Librarianship', Hyperlinked library, Library Advocacy) can help librarians build on their LIS training and explore new areas of the profession. Librarians can develop MOOCs as a professional development tool through conducting seminar, workshop, conference, writing article in library journals etc. According to Stepens, the experiment on MOOCs will help to procedure "a professional development model for a librarian that is open and free and becomes a community of learners coming from library schools and jobs".

MOOCS IN LIBRARY & INFORMATION SCIENCE

The MOOCs like in other areas have made a beginning in LIS. A course on 'New Librarianship', Hyperlinked library, Library Advocacy Unshushed had started. There is a scope to run such courses in LIS and interest among library professionals and students in taking MOOCs.

MOOCS IMPACT ON LIS EDUCATION IN DEVELOPING COUNTRIES

The professionals and students from developing countries would immensely get benefitted from such initiatives as quality education in many such countries is still a dream. It may also give a chance for retired and talented professionals (including teachers) to independently develop lectures and offer courses online. For example a retired Professor (or Librarian) may share his wealth of knowledge and experiences through MOOCs sitting from the comforts of his home encasing on brand equity and may also earn some extra money. Some of the following implications would certainly benefit the learners from developing countries.

- Helping in raising the profile of a teacher, school and university & low or no tuition fees
- Collaboration with national and international library schools and open online courses
- Option of selecting courses from different and elite schools/universities (Choice based courses)

THE ROLE OF LIBRARIES AND LIBRARIANS

There have been high levels of attention in recent months given to the academic "faces" of MOOC platforms and the instructors that deliver the MOOCs themselves. There is a little documentary evidence about the role of libraries and librarians in relation to the development of the MOOC movement. MOOCs are different and require the re-planning and repositioning of the library service. The librarian must put every facility in the way of the readers so that they shall be led on from good to better. Restructuring the library and its staff to turn them into consultants in a culture of collaboration put librarians on more of an equal footing, enabling them to better collaborate with colleagues in faculties. Through developing the role as a consultant, librarians can take advantage of their unique position & operate within the same educational establishment whilst maintaining an external objective view of the MOOC and its possible content. The second step is to raise awareness of the skills, knowledge, and experience of librarians that can be readily adapted for to accommodate MOOC production.

THE ISSUES AND CHALLENGES FOR MOOCS:

Over recent years there has been a significant change in the societal adoption of Internet technologies with extensive proliferation and use in more economically developed countries. However, in terms of the proliferation of MOOCs as an educational approach, there is a risk that the current enthusiasm is being driven by a self-selecting group of highly educated, IT literate individuals who are able to navigate the sometimes complex, confusing and intimidating nature of online learning. In general, there are concerns about the pedagogy and quality of current MOOC courses, with a clear distinction between process and content-based approaches. The motivation for some MOOCs is a philanthropic one and for others a business proposition. However, in both cases, there is the challenge of finding a viable model that allows for sustainability of MOOC provision.

There are a number of challenges that librarians will face as MOOCs take off. These include:

- Influencing faculties, Copyright and licensing;
- Delivering remote services, and Diverse demographics and scale

MOOCS IN INDIA AND THE FUTURE GOAL

In India MOOCs is not familiar, the students taking

the MOOC courses were found to be very non-traditional but were mainly concentrated in the English-speaking countries. Moreover, due to the flexible nature of the courses, MOOC has become quite a hit among working professionals as well. Another major reason why MOOC has become increasingly popular among Indian students is their aspiration level to pursue courses from top universities abroad. Indian students have welcomed MOOCs with open arms.

Future

- MOOC will be folded as a regular resource & having its own audience
- MOOC will stand as supplementary income sources. & interact with mobile
- MOOC will help to improve educational outcomes & to encourage innovation in teaching, learning and research in future.

Goals

- Extend the reach of the institution to a wider audience and improve access to education.
- Build and maintain brand & To improve the economics of higher education
- Improving educational outcomes has been achieved through MOOCs
- innovation in teaching, learning and research

SUGGESTIONS

- LIS education/ libraries may be produced by LIS journals and proper marketing of thematic issue should be done on MOOCs and get involve in MOOCs movement.
- Prominent and new authors may be approached and encouraged to write articles on MOOCs for LIS education.

- More scholarly articles, special issues on MOOCs and LIS education/ libraries should be published by leading Indian LIS journals/ magazines & more seminar, conference, refresher courses organized by different LIS schools of India and different libraries.
- LIS professionals should take initiatives, opportunities and challenges to get involved in MOOCs movement.

LIBRARIES AND MOOCS

Librarians were not involved earlier in the development of MOOCs. Later on, librarians responded by offering online chat services, blogs, email reference, accessibility through numerous forms of social media interactivity & support tools such as LibGuides Librarians have the ability to evolve, due to emerging technologies and ever-shifting educational landscapes.

- To introduce MOOC in Campus & Orientation to students for adaptation of MOOC
- To play the role of teacher & to develop digital literacy skill librarian has to provide support to students who are enrolled for MOOC.

INITIATIVES TAKEN BY INDIAN GOVERNMENT & INSTITUTIONS FOR MOOCS

Many initiatives have been taken by the Indian Government for Open Course Education.

- Sakshat, EDUSAT Consortium For Educational Communication (CEC),
- National Digital Repository of IGNOU, ERNET, Shishya (XI-XII Standards,
- CBSE Board), Vidya Vahini (School Teacher and Students), e-PG-Pathshala, Apana Course, NPTEL, SWAYAM & GIAN.
- Birla Institute of Technology and Sciences (BITS) collaborated with MIT & Harvard

- International Crops Research Institute for the Semi-Arid Tropics (ICRISAT)
- Visvesvaraya Technological University (VTU)

ADVANTAGES OF MOOCS

- Innovative startups, top colleges and other reputable institutions have made a huge range of top-quality education available through MOOCs.
- Many of these courses are completely free in order to broadly avail education.
- MOOCs have flexibility and don't need any special qualifications to register for a MOOC.
- Typically you just have to sign up with a few basic details and ready to get started.

DISADVANTAGES OF MOOCS

- One downside of MOOCs is that they usually aren't accredited, which of course makes them less valuable for your career.
- The MOOC versions of college courses are often simplified and may not match the level of the real thing.
- A caveat that's gotten a lot of attention as the MOOC trend has progressed is the sometimes massive tendency towards course abandonment.
- Another demerit of MOOCs is the lack of interaction with your professor.

edX Source	2012	Harvard MIT professors	Certificate	Mix & nominal charges for certi-fication	edX open source & non-profit delivery platform, research outcomes	60 million dollar from Harvard & MIT	edX open videos
e-PG pathashala	2014	Subject expert		free	Covering 71 subjects at post graduate level	MHRD under national mission ICT	Textual Documents uploaded in some subjects
NPTEL online	2014	IIT professor	Certificate	Mix (nominal charge for certi-ficate)	Massive online data in engineering subjects, quality faculty of IITs	Joint institutes of IITs & IISs, funded by MHRD	1 month to 5 months certification program, good quality video
IIT Delhi	2013	IIT professor	Certificate	free	Free exam & certification on accomplishment of course	Coursera	Video lectures, prerequisite, forum
IIT Mumbai	2014	IIT professor	Certificate	Mix (nominal charge for certificate)	First Indian MOOC Launchedon edX platform	Harvard & MIT	6-12 week short term programs, three online video forum
myBskool	2014	Professor	Certificate	Paid	UGC accredited	Think Big Edu-	Online video

	from IITs & IIMs & subject experts		program, domain specific program Govt of India certified program	venture Pvt Ltd	lecturer
Apna Course	Subject experts	Certificate depend on program	Signature track, global certification, self paced course, life time validity course.	Spearhead edu online pvt Ltd	Video lecturers and textbook material

CONCLUSION

The emergence of MOOCs represents a rising trend of removing the learning process from the physical campus but to an exaggerated degree. OOCs are making a huge impact on distance education. Large enrolment numbers clearly provide proof of that. MOOCs offer to open up higher education by providing informal, Indian governments are in process to create MOOCs in higher education through e-PG Pathshala. Working people and housewives who cannot join regular education, MOOCs provide a learning opportunity to them for educate from their desired universities. To make LIS MOOC requires onus support from Ministry of Culture, States' Minister of Culture, Raja Rammohun Roy Library Foundation, National Mission on Libraries, INFLIBNET, Department of Library Science and Library Association of respective states is must. It is a duty to librarians to create more awareness among reader's community. Though, librarians are the torch bearer and face value of these valued sources. As academic libraries invest more time, energy, and resources in the OER movement, continued momentum in the open access scholarly publishing area is vital as well.

REFERENCES

1. Allen, I. E. and Seaman, J. (2013). Changing Course: ten years of tracking online education in the United States.
2. Bond, P. & Leibowitz,F. (2013). MOOCs and Serials. Serials Review, 39(4), 258-260.
3. Creed-Dikeogu, G. & Clark, C. (2013). Are you MOOC-ing yet? A review for academic libraries. Kansas Library Association College and University Libraries Section Proceedings, 3(1), 9-13.
4. Cheverie, Joan. "MOOCs an Intellectual Property: Ownership and Use Rights". Retrieved 18 April 2013.
5. Daniel, J. (2012). Making sense of MOOCs: Musing in a maze of myth, paradox and possibility. Journal of Interactive Media in Education, 3.
6. David F Carr (20 August 2013). "Udacity hedges on open licensing for MOOCs". Information Week. Retrieved 21 August 2013.
7. Educause (2013b). Copyright challenges in a MOOC

environment. Retrieved from https://net.educause.edu/ir/library/pdf/PUB9014.pdf.

8. Edward Island. Retrieved from http://www.elearnspace.org/Articles/MOOC_Final.pdf.

9. Frederiksen, L. (2013). Makers and MOOCs. Public Services Quarterly, 9(2), 157-161.

10. Massis, B.E. (2013). MOOCs and the library. New Library World, 114 (5/6), 267 – 270.

11. McAulay, A., Stewart, B., & Siemens, G. (2010). The MOOC model for digital practice. University of Prince.

12. Nahak, B. (2016). E-Resources of Web Discovery Tools and Services in Digital Libraries: Modern Trends in Library & Information Science in Digital Environment/Kishore, Amit(ed), Karn,S.K.,Das. B.K & Chaudhury, K.K.University Press: Agra.

13. Yuan, L. and Powell, S. (2013a). MOOCs and open education: Implications for higher education. JISCCETIS, Retrieved from http://jisc.cetis.ac.uk/

17

Changing Role of Libraries and Information Professionals

Kiran Prakash Bachchhav
Librarian,
Sarvajanik Shikshan Sanstha's Adv.V.B. Deshpande College of Commerce (Night) Mulund (West), Mumbai- 400080, Maharashtra

ABSTRACT

The advent of information and communication technology has changed the whole world. Libraries and Librarians are also not exceptions for this change. Information technology paved the way for new technologies entering the library. Libraries have converted itself from physical to virtual libraries. Librarians have also adopted this technological change for the library. This paper focuses on changing the role of libraries and librarians due to the advent of information and communication technologies in libraries.

Keywords : Libraries, Information Technology, OPAC, Librarians, Role of Information Professionals

INTRODUCTION

The library is the historic paradigm of information storage and retrieval. Similarly, publishing is a paradigm for information market. Now both library and publishing are on the frontline of changes. The change is not just superficial but these fields are changing because of technology, dependency for management and service provision. The change is far deeper. Earlier, libraries were customers of publishers but now libraries can be partners of publishers because information is provided for a price. Librarians are getting more negotiating powers. Concepts like public lending rights are being introduced. There are three strands of information.

Public Information

This is the information in public domain which means it is publically available within the limits of copyright laws and other legal bindings and commerce.

Personal Information

This is about individual information. For example, patient's record, insurance records, bank transactions etc. privacy is there but it can bypass or accused under special circumstances.

Private Information

This information is not meant for public circulation. It is gathered and stored for a private purpose. It includes office files, information about the competitors. This information is stored in different ways and also used in a different manner.

CHANGING ROLE OF LIBRARIES

The library building is no longer remaining the boundary. A library can be extended beyond the four walls of the library. It has become virtual now. Users can access information from laboratories, classrooms and hostel rooms, even from their home with internet connection. Such things are mostly seen in IIT and IIM campuses. Students are accessing e-journals from remote places.

- Traditional catalogue cards and cabinet are being replaced by OPAC's and web OPAC's because it occupies less space compared to traditional catalogues, because of internet connectivity it can be accessed from anywhere and anytime, it is available 24X7, many people can refer or access it at the same time, in OPAC even if the reader knows one or two words in the title then he can find the required document. But in the conventional catalogue, unless you know the first word in the title or exact author name, it is not possible to locate the book. OPAC is more flexible.

- The new mediums such as CD's, DVD's, VCD's etc. are entering the library. As a result, people with new skills such as system managers, maintenance engineer, resident engineer and programmers have to be introduced in addition to librarians.
- Libraries have become computerizes now. Various commercial and open source software are available which are used to put complete library collection in the software. Libraries depend on their financial conditions, are approaching for these software. All the collection of the library is now available on OPAC.
- Electronic journals, e-archives etc. have been introduced to save space, shelves, binding and photocopies. Libraries are subscribing various databases related to different subjects. There is log in ID and password is given to every student. So students can access these databases from anywhere and anytime.
- Document delivery is done faster using the internet. A scanned image can be immediately sent. A lot of money can be saved on postage and courier services.
- Information Technology has transformed the work of libraries and librarians. There are more of multi-professional aspects (computer skills, legal knowledge about copyright etc.)
- There are newer technologies and new challenges are developing to meet the users need. The Internet has

entered the libraries in a big way.

- In this technological world, security should be maintained. Many libraries have approached for new technologies such as RFID, OR code, Barcode etc. to secure libraries from book theft.
- Intranet, meta-resources such as portals and subject gateways, metadata, MARC 21, doubling core, Z39.50, XML are some of the new technologies being employed.
- Two or more number of libraries are coming together to form union catalogues and consortia's just to meet their user's need. Here student can access catalogue of all other libraries to get required document with the help of document delivery service.
- While new skills are being introduced, some of the old skills are still required as the curricular getting more and more emphasis on technology-centered subjects.
- Libraries are getting de-institutionalize. As a result, the concept of library as a location, building or as a meeting place is disappearing. There are virtual libraries such as librarywala.com, British Council etc. were one need not go to these libraries physically. People can select books using web OPAC's, book demand is sent through mail and books are delivered through courier services. Thus, libraries becoming a network of information than a place. Some old skills are re-appearing under new names such as customer care.

CHANGING ROLE OF LIBRARIANS/INFORMATION PROFESSIONALS

Librarians are traditionally information professionals. They collect, organize (classification, cataloguing abstracting, indexing etc.), stored, retrieved and disseminate information. In this process, librarians manage financial, human and information resources. Therefore the provision of information is the role played by librarians. There are many changes in the role played by librarians. Quality of service is more in focus. Quality of service is measured by speed (response time) & accuracy (precise subject). Quality is not measured by a number of books in the library or number of book loans, therefore the earlier indicators such as the number of books and number of loans are no longer measuring quality. It is only response time and accuracy which will decide the quality of a library. The librarian's role as a custodian is fading out. No doubt the importance is given to the preservation and promoting information. Therefore today, it is more important to access the information than to possess the information.

There are new roles taken up by librarians. Many of the new names for library professionals are actually the need and sometimes these different names are just to draw the attention. Apart from the traditional designations of the librarians such as Librarian, Assistant Librarian, University Librarian, Deputy Librarian etc. some new designations have been emerging. These new designations are given according to the workflow and background of concern institution/ department etc. Following are some of the new roles and designations of the librarians.

Knowledge Mediator

It took librarians beyond cataloguing and in-house resources. Librarian has to be more technosavy. There are so many websites are available on various subjects with many more topics. Librarian has to choose, select, organized, preserve and disseminate only that information which is suitable and required for its users. Otherwise, due to information overload, it is very difficult to choose the exact information.

Knowledge Preserver

This designation included digital and electronic information which required a policy, strategy and knowledge of copyright. By abiding all the rules and regulation, librarians are preserving all formats of information for the future generation. Each and every information is useful for the users like present generation, future generation should also take advantage of this information for their study purpose.

Information Architect

In this role, the librarian has to map information related to different sources on similar subjects just as an architect does with space. Librarian has to be perfect while mapping the information because finally, he has to decide which information from which source is fit for that subject.

Information Gatekeeper

Here librarian functions as a middleman who deals with information providers and information consumers. Librarian's role here is to take required information from the providers and to give this information to the user in less time.

Cybrarian

Suppose to perform the activities which a librarian does with printed resources. However, the main difference is cybrarian deals with information storage in cyberspace. Cybrarian makes available the required information on the demand by users.

Hybrid Librarian

It is multimedia centre with different media resources. Within hybrid librarianship there are different names depending on the medium of resources. Because of technology, many of the methods of functioning in the library have changed. For example: ordering books, subscribing the journals, price verification, claims of non-arrivals have all become online activities.

Ordering : Library can buy a book from an internet bookseller by money transactions done electronically.

Subscription of Journals : Is done through consortia and journals are received electronically. As a result, paper cost is much more eliminated, postage is eliminated and losses in transit are avoided. So, there is no question of not arrival. E-archiving of journals will lead to space saving and also expenditure on the binding.

Reference Librarian

Most of the academic and reference libraries are having this post. Here librarian takes care of the books which are not textbooks but reference books.

Research assistant

This designation sometimes creates confusion but it is the post of librarian itself but due to a different atmosphere, the designation is different. Institutions/government departments related to science and technology are having such post.

Scientific Assistant

Science & technological institutions/government/ autonomous institutions are having this post. Here work is quite similar but the way of doing work like in traditional libraries is different.

Documentalist/Documentation Officer

Documentation officer is the designation most commonly found in corporate libraries which are mostly related to commerce, civil engineering, architecture firms etc. Here way of working of the librarian is mostly related to desktop work.

CONCLUSION

Information technology has brought the whole world together. Every field has the glimpses of technology. Libraries are adopting new technologies to provide its users quick service in less time. Librarians are becoming more technical in order to bring all the useful information for the users at one place. Users are accessing their libraries by sitting at home. Technology has reduced the workload in the libraries. Information technology with its adaptation in the library has completely changed the atmosphere of the library and information professionals.

REFERENCE

1. Bridges, K. Ed. Expectations of Librarians in the 21st Century. Westport, Greenwood Press, 2003.
2. Brophy, P. The Library in the 21st Century – New Services for the Information Age. London, Library Association, 2001.
3. Martin, William J. Global Information Society. 2nd ed. London, ASLIB, 1996.

18

Total Quality Management in Libraries

Jagjit Singh
Librarian, Doaba College,
Tanda Road, Jalandhar City-144004, Punjab

ABSTRACT

Total Quality Management in libraries is a very important aspect of the libraries. TQM is a continuous process which is linked in term of quantity and quality resources and services in the libraries. The role of TQM is changing with the passage of time due to ICT techniques, now libraries are providing a large number of services which required TQM in libraries. This paper will discuss how TQM is essential in the libraries.

Keywords : TQM, Resources, Services, Libraries, Users'

INTRODUCTION

In the recent years functioning of the libraries are changing due to users expectations, information explosion, ICT techniques, electronic resources etc. libraries are the service provider which provide a large number of resources and service for their users. All the library services like acquisition, technical, periodical, circulation is available for the users for satisfying their demands; the whole service can be fully beneficial if the quality is available for the users. This process involves Total Quality Management which satisfies user's expectation according to their demands. TQM is generally customer focused approach which satisfies customer requirement with quality services by the parent organization through their employees. TQM term was firstly introduced in Japan. In libraries, TQM is very appropriate because libraries are service based part of any organization that provides a variety of services by their employees. In ICT environment libraries are more concerned with TQM because in information explosion era user may not be able to recognize relevancy or authenticity of the resource which may be available in print or electronic form, therefore libraries any play very important role for delivering right information for the right user in the right time, the whole process may be successful only through TQM.

TOTAL QUALITY MANAGEMENT CONCEPT

TQM involves three components

1. Quality
2. Staff Involvement
3. Users satisfaction

Any organization success is depending on above three components. Firstly quality is necessary for establishing in the market; staff involvement is compulsory for delivering the services and the last and ultimate goal is users' satisfaction. If above three components succeed successfully then any organization can achieve their targets and the whole process must be achieved by the policies of the management. In libraries quality resources/ documents/information are necessary for the libraries; second proper staff involvement is required for delivering the right information at the right user in the right time; and finally and the ultimate goal is users satisfaction with library resources and services is essential.

FEATURES OF TOTAL QUALITY MANAGEMENT

All resources and services in the library must be screened in the quality manner than the quantity manner.

Main features of TQM are:

Usability of the resources and services : All library resources and services must be usable. Library staff must consider all the users to motivate for the use of all resources and services of the library with providing a description.

Proper Display of all resources and services : TQM should be more effective if each and every resource and service of the library must be proper display.

Selectivity of resources and services : In TQM selection of resources and services is playing a very important role. Therefore librarian must take proper consideration for selection of resources and services.

Dissemination of resources and services : Dissemination of resources and service are playing a very important role in TQM for providing right resources and services to the right users at the right time.

Maintenance : In TQM maintenance is required for proper reuse of library resources and services for the users of the library.

Time Management : TQM requires time management for the proper use of library resources and services; if library users' expectation fulfilled on time with required information then objective of TQM should be fulfilled.

User satisfaction : TQM objective is to satisfy users' expectation, therefore, library staff should be able to provide all required information in a proper manner and on time for achieving the objective of TQM.

NEED OF TQM IN LIBRARIES

Following are the main points which recognize TQM in libraries:

Users' satisfaction : This is first and important point for any organization particularly for libraries is users' satisfaction. Libraries are the services agencies which are always linked to users. Therefore users' satisfaction is the main objects of the library.

Image of the Libraries : TQM is connected with the images of the libraries; if any library is to provide better resources and services to its users then the image of the library is brightened among the users: this is only possible if TQM should be applicable in the library.

Best among the libraries : TQM required in the libraries because quality services should be provided in the TQM environment and best title among the libraries is only possible through the TQM.

Proper Usage of Library Resources and Services : Library resources and services should be used only; if it applies TQM; therefore TQM should encourage libraries to the proper use of its resources and services among the library users.

Every User is important : TQM recognize the importance of single users; if any user is satisfied in the library by its resources and services then the motive of the library is achieved.

Spirit of Team Work : TQM emphasis on teamwork; it recognized the role of every staff member in entire work of the library.

Welcome to New Technology : TQM always welcome of new technology; therefore it easy the work of the library and more useful for the staff and its user.

Stress on Improvement : TQM always stresses on the improvement of the quality of resources and services, therefore, it is more suitable for the libraries which are regularly engaged in providing quality services to their users.

Full Participation : TQM gives consideration to the full participation of its staff members and its users; therefore it is beneficial for the improvement of the library.

Competition : TQM believes in competition in quality services; libraries are also worked in competitive environment in term of its resources and service; every library wants to give maximum resources and services to its users. It creates healthy competition among the libraries.

To Enhance Users Awareness : TQM always enhances user awareness with its quality resources and services; libraries also fall in this category so TQM is needed in the libraries.

TOTAL QUALITY MANAGEMENT REQUIRED IN LIBRARIES

TQM concept for libraries is not new; libraries are providing users oriented services. TQM is providing a platform for library resources and services in a new manner for the maximum utilization of its resources and services by their users. TQM includes theory and practice; it emphasis on practice than the theoretical work. TQM recognizes human feelings; if human feelings are satisfied with the resources and services then automatically resources and services of the library should be used day by day. Library users are the real public who expands the publicity of library resources and services among the new users of the library. TQM suggest and improve library resources and services for providing better facilities to its users. TQM should focus on;

- Users satisfaction
- Proper training of library staff
- Proper communication among the staff and users
- To engage participation of library staff as a tea
- To adopt new technologies for more improvement in resources and services of the library
- Feedback from staff and library users

Above points are very important for libraries to achieve TQM. TQM is a continuous process which always required proper feedback for providing better services to its users. In libraries, each and every resource and services should be available for its users and maximum attention to its proper maintenance. The library should develop a mechanism that provides the latest information of new resources and services introduced by the library for their users. Users' interest and consciousness must be considered when any resource is purchased for the library. TQM demands strong leadership which can play a very important role to achieve the organization goal. Leadership should consider each aspect of the library, staff and users point of view. Leadership must focus on users whose satisfaction is much more concerned in the library.

TQM IMPACT ON LIBRARIES

TQM can play a very important role in libraries. It has various impacts on libraries like;

Improvement of Quality Based Resources and Services : TQM always focused on quality based resources and services, therefore, improvement is always available in TQM. Libraries should be guided in the TQM concept and should provide quality services to their users.

Fulfillment of Users Expectations : TQM recognize the users' expectations; libraries are more concerned with the fulfilment of users' expectations, therefore, TQM is helpful in this direction.

Importance of Human values : TQM respect human values; its impact clearly reflect the functioning of the library. Human is very sensitive if he/she realize library realize its existence then their progress is automatically improved.

Collection of the Library : TQM is concerned with quality then a collection of the library should be qualitative with the guidance of TQM.

Full Devotion : TQM demand full devotion of the staff and users; therefore its impact on libraries show the clear picture of the successfulness of the library.

Accuracy : TQM demands accuracy in the services which are very beneficial from the library point of view.

Feedback : TQM required proper feedback which is also helpful for improving the weakness of the organization; in libraries, feedback is also helpful for improving library services to their users.

HURDLES FOR IMPLEMENTING TQM IN LIBRARIES

There are many hurdles for implementing TQM in libraries;

Finance : Finance is always a big problem for almost all libraries to provide quality services to their users. A large number of organizations don't want to spend more funds on the libraries. At this time it is a very big problem for almost all the libraries.

Lack of Infrastructure : TQM requires proper infrastructure to provide quality services to their users. A large number of libraries are facing this problem. This is a big hurdle among the libraries to implement TQM.

Lack of Training of Library Staff : TQM demands trained staff in the libraries, but the reality is that a large number of libraries are facing the shortage of library staff and available staff is not familiar with ICT and don't want to familiar with the ICT.

Support of the Authorities : TQM requires the support of the authorities for implementing qualitative services for their users; authorities are not supporting due to finance, they don't spend more funds on the libraries.

Lack of Planning and initiative : Implementation of TQM in libraries depends upon the proper planning and initiative of the organization. A large number of libraries are not able to implement above points. Therefore it is a big hurdle for implementing TQM in libraries.

CONCLUSION

At the end we conclude that TQM is very important in libraries for improving library resources and services; but in real picture, libraries are facing many problems like finance, lack of infrastructure, lack of training etc. TQM can change the functioning of the libraries in a better way and can fulfill users' expectations and can also be helpful for library staff.

REFERENCES

1. Ahluwalia, J. S. (2001). Total quality management: Creating a quality environment for the next millennium. New Delhi, Vanity Bks. International.
2. Bankapur, V. And Mansur, S. (2001). TQM for library and information system, University News, vol. 39 (28), pp. 8-10.
3. Charantimath Poornima, M. (2006). Total quality management. Noida: Pearson education.
4. Dodrajka, Sangeeta. (2007). Total quality management: text and cases. New Delhi, Deep & Deep Publications.
5. Kanji, G. K. and Asher, M. (1993). Total quality management process: systematic approach. Madras, Productivity.
6. Lal, H. (1990). Total quality management: A practical approach. New Delhi, Wiley Eastern Ltd.
7. Mandal, S. K. (2005). Total quality management. New Delhi: Vikas.
8. Mustafa, A. (2011). Total quality management. Delhi, Manglam Publishers.
9. Shukla, Rajesh Kumar. (2006). Total quality management: practising manager. Lucknow, New Royal Book Co.
10. Sundra Raju, S. M. (1995). Total Quality Management: A primer. New Delhi, Tata McGraw-Hill, Ind.

19

Research Performance on Phytochemistry Literature in India: A Scientometric Profile

Chandran Velmurugan
Research Scholar
Department of Library and Information Science, Periyar University, Salem- 636 011, Tamilnadu
Natarajan Radhakrishnan
Associate Professor
Department of Library and Information Science, Periyar University, Salem- 636 011, Tamilnadu

ABSTRACT

This chapter deals with the observations of research publications in the field of Phytochemistry in India as reflected from the Web of Science (WoS) core collection database during 1994-2014. The purpose of this paper is to observe the various parameters such as authorship pattern, single vs. joint - authored research publications, International collaboration, Institution-based collaboration, subject based categories, and most cited references, ranking of core journals, highly cited authors, papers and productive keywords through the scholarly publications. For analysis, a total 1280 scholarly publications with 1216 citations and 2083 cited references were found and have retrieved in worldwide. 121 research outputs with 1446 citations and 473 authors and the cited references are 8732 were collected in the time span of 21 years from India. The findings of the study reveal that the highest number of research articles (=148, 11.6%) were published in 2014 throughout the world and the majority of Indian literature (=28, 23.1%) were produced in 201 l. The highest number of articles (=7, 5.8%) with 70 global citations published by the 'Father Muller Med College' and the same articles with 108 global citations and it is found that the word 'Review' has 36 record counts with 409 total citations and has placed in the first rank and followed by the word 'Phytochemistry' has 33 record counts with 655 citations and ranked in the second position.

Keywords : Phytochemistry, scientometrics, publication analysis, research trends, h-index, g-index, e-index, hc-index, WoS, India.

INTRODUCTION

The term 'Phytochemistry' has defined 'the branch of chemistry dealing with the chemical processes associated with plant life and the chemical compounds produced by plants' (http://www.yourdictionary.com/phytochemistry). According to Merriam-Webster dictionary, defined 'the chemistry of plants, plant processes, and plant products' (http://www.merriam-webster.com/dictionary/phytochemistry). Phytochemistry, or the chemistry of plants, one of the early subdivisions of organic chemistry, has been of great importance in the identification of plant substances of medicinal importance (Oxford online dictionary). The branch of organic chemistry dealing with the chemistry of plants (http://www.wordfind.com).

To identify the progress and development of recent trends of Phytochemistry research performance and also to support and strengthen this Phytochemistry field, researchers have taken into attention this topic to estimate and scrutinize the analysis by means of scientometric observations. The scientometric analysis is employed by the research scientists to study the growth of scientific publications in given science field specifically. This study is based on the bibliographic analysis which was first used the term by Pritchard (1969) as the application of statistical and mathematical methods to books and other communications. As this scientometric research is one of the emerging thrust areas of research in the electronic knowledge world, integrating several branches of human knowledge.

RELATED WORK

A number of scientometric as well as bibliometric studies have already done by various researchers and scientists in different subjects for past few decades. Mallikand Mandal(2013) reported the literature outputs and collaborative structure analyzing microRNA for the year 2002 to 2012. The results reveal that the annual growth of countries was 36.60% and institutions were 76.64%, journals was 64.80% and the research areas was 30.5%. The average number of research papers per author was increased in first three years and after that, it was decreased gradually. The USA topped the list and followed by China in mircoRNA research. Shao et al. (2013) studied the scientometric analysis in oncology literature during 2001-2010. The author has selected 30 oncology journals data were collected from the web of science database. Based on the analysis, it was identified that the primary research centres and noticed the top 20 institutions in oncology. Yu et al (2012) described the scientific publications in the field of photosynthesis for the year 1992-2009. The data was collected through web of science (WoS) Science Citation Index Expanded (SCI-Expanded). The findings show that the study involved in terms of research outputs, form-wise manuscripts, subject-wise, language-wise, country–wise and institution–wise outputs. The study identified that climate change; water, stress, nitrogen and carbon dioxide were the hot topics of research on photosynthesis. Aswathy and Gopikuttan (2012) have carried out the single journal study in the Journal of Spacecraft and Rockets which was published by American

Institute of Aeronautics and Astronautics for the period between 2006 and 2010. This study covered 780 literature output and 15648 references. The analysis includes various factors such as research growth rate, the proportion of authorship trends, length of papers, distribution based on the subject, institutions, and collaborative countries. The scientometric indicators such as degree of collaboration, Lotka's law were also applied to test the author productivity. It is found that most of the journal articles published from the USA as the origin of this journal and the multi-authored papers were majority than the single authors.

To support and strengthen the current research, authors' early works have chosen and the works dealt with in terms of authorship pattern, collaborative research work in Library Herald (Velmurugan and Radhakrishnan, 2015), Journal of Intellectual Property Rights (Velmurugan, 2014, 2015), Indian Journal of Pure and Applied Physics (Velmurugan, 2014), Annals of Library and Information Studies (Velmurugan, 2013), in DESIDOC Journal of Library and Information Technology (Velmurugan and Radhakrishnan, 2015), publication research trends in Webology (Velmurugan, 2015), in IETE Technical Review Journal (Velmurugan and Radhakrishnan, 2014), in Journal of Intellectual Property Rights (Velmurugan, 2014), Indian Journal of Pure and Applied Physics (Velmurugan, 2014), Indian Journal of Biotechnology (Velmuruganand Radhakrishnan, 2014), research productivity of Amylase in Microbiology in Indian Perspective(Velmuruganand Radhakrishnan, 2015), Literature output of Plagiarism (Velmurugan and Radhakrishnan, 2015), in Journal of Information Literacy (Velmurugan, and Radhakrishnan, 2015) and quantitative analysis of scientific publications Output on Engineering Journal (Velmuruganand Radhakrishnan, 2015), Literature output of Supply Chain Management (Velmuruganand Radhakrishnan, 2015).

SOURCE DATA OF PHYTOCHEMISTRY IN INDIA

The source data of Phytochemistry in India has been investigated by the researchers using the Publish or Perish (PoP) software in terms of year –wise total number of papers, citations, papers per author, authors per paper, h-index, g-index, e-index, hc-index, hI-index, hI,norm, hI,annual, hm-index, AW-index, AWCR and AWCRpA etc. the Table 1 illustrate the whole details of source data of Phytochemistry. This type of effort has already been done by the same authors in Pharmacognosy research as reflected in the Web of Science in Advances in Pharmacognosy and Phytomedicine Velmurugan& Radhakrishnan(2015).

S.No.	*Item Details*	*Description*
1	Source topic	Phytochemistry
2	Geographical area	INDIA
3	Database	Web of Science Core Collection
4	Query date	2015-12-08
5	Papers	121
6	Citations	1446
7	Years	21 (1994-2014)
8	Cites/year	68.86
9	Cites/paper	11.95/2.0/0 (mean/median/mode)
10	Cites/author	354.66
11	Cites/author/year	16.88
12	Papers/author	38.69
13	Authors/paper	3.91/3.0/3 (mean/median/mode)
14	h-index	18 (79%)
15	g-index	36 (91%)
16	e-index	28.57
17	hc-index	16
18	hI-index	3.31
19	hI,norm	8
20	hI,annual	0.38
21	hm-index	7.81

22	AW-index	16.09
23	AWCR	258.73
24	AWCRpA	73.20
25	Hirsch a=4.46, m=0.86	
26	Contemporary ac=4.04	

MATERIALS AND METHOD

For Phytochemistry publication analysis, researchers have selected the web of science database and retrieved a total of 1280 world publication outputs during the period from between 1994 to 2014. Researchers refined the geographical area and chosen the country 'INDIA' and retrieved the available data of one hundred and twenty one (=121) literature outputs with 1446 total global citations (TGCS) and 8732 cited references (CR)from 60 core journals by 473 total authors in India collaborated with only 17 countries for the period of 21 years. To estimate the research output based on the data, the following scientometric tools have been employed for this analysis to retrieve the better results for the study. The tools such as Degree of Collaboration (DC), Compound annual growth rate (CAGR), Growth Models such as Liner Growth Model, Exponential Growth Model and Logarithmic Growth Model and R2 Value for publications of Phytochemistry in India.

DATA ANALYSIS AND RESULTS

Comparative growth analysis of research papers between World and India

Table 1 and Figure 1-2 bring out the growth pattern of research productivity between World and India in Phytochemistry for the year 1989-2014. The results mirror that maximum number of scientific papers more than three digits (=118 articles) were published from all over the World in 2011 whereas in Indian literature outputs more than two digits (13 articles) were produced in 2010. The highest number of research articles (=148, 11.6%) were published in

2014 throughout the world and the majority of Indian literature (=28, 23.1%) were produced in 201 l. It is identified from the Table 1 based on the papers in India, the colossal number of (= 28, 23.17%) articles were published in 2011 and the least number of papers (=5 and below) were found almost before 2008 and the nil number of publications in the year 2008. The growth rate is gradually increased except 2009 in terms of world productivity and the growth rate is slightly decreased compared with world literature in Phytochemistry during the study period.

Table 1. Growth analysis of research papers

Sl. No	*PY*	*World*		*India*	
		TP	*TP%*	*TP*	*TP%*
1	1989	3	0.2	-	-
2	1990	3	0.2	-	-
3	1991	6	0.5	-	-
4	1992	18	1.4	-	-
5	1993	18	1.4	-	-
6	1994	21	1.6	2	1.7
7	1995	26	2.0	-	-
8	1996	28	2.2	-	-
9	1997	36	2.8	2	1.7
10	1998	28	2.2	-	-
11	1999	27	2.1	1	0.8
12	2000	29	2.3	-	-
13	2001	34	2.7	-	-
14	2002	26	2.0	-	-
15	2003	36	2.8	2	1.7
16	2004	32	2.5	3	2.5
17	2005	35	2.7	2	1.7
18	2006	41	3.2	1	0.8
19	2007	81	6.3	5	4.1
20	2008	70	5.5	-	-
21	2009	58	4.5	6	5.0
22	2010	84	6.6	13	10.7

23	2011	118	9.2	28	23.1
24	2012	114	8.9	16	13.2
25	2013	160	12.5	18	14.9
26	2014	148	11.6	22	18.2
		1280	100	121	100

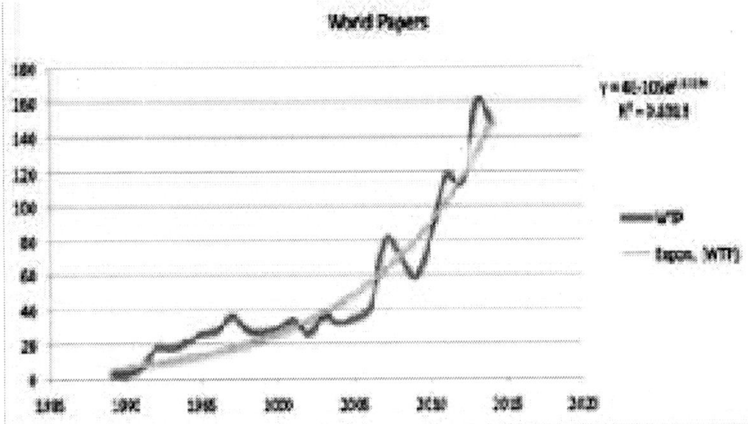

Fig. 1. World Literature output

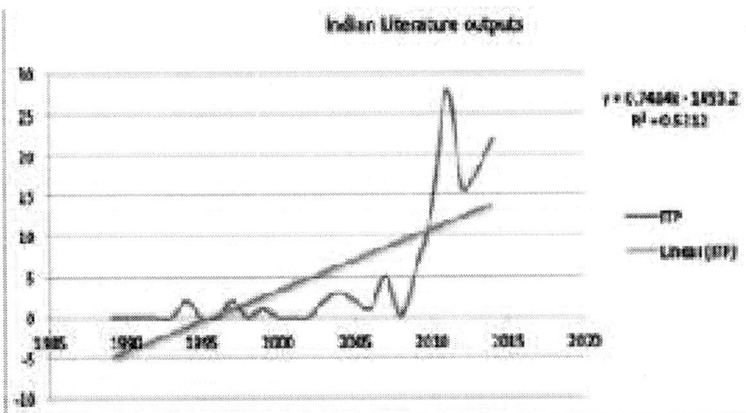

Fig. 2. Literature output-India

The trend line analysis has been to determine the exponential and linear values of world and Indian literature outputs in Phytochemistry. Therefore, researchers identified the exponential growth value of world literature output is y = 4E-105e0.1219x, and the R^2 value is 0.8319. The Indian output of linear trend line value is y = 0.7484x - 1493.2, and the R^2 value is 0.5312.

Form-wise publication

Manuscripts are classified in terms of articles, review, article based on proceedings paper, correction, editorial materials, notes, short communications, and abstract etc. For the present study, researchers are taken all types of documents which are available in the web of science bibliographic database during the period of study. In this context, Figure 3 indicates that the data such as research articles (=61, 257 citations) 50.4 percent, review (=57, 1186 citations) 47.1 percent, articles from proceeding papers, correction, editorial materials are each one records (0.8%) respectively. The results bring out that most of the documents are research articles (=50.4%) and placed in the first rank and based on the citations review articles are in the first rank (=1186 citations).

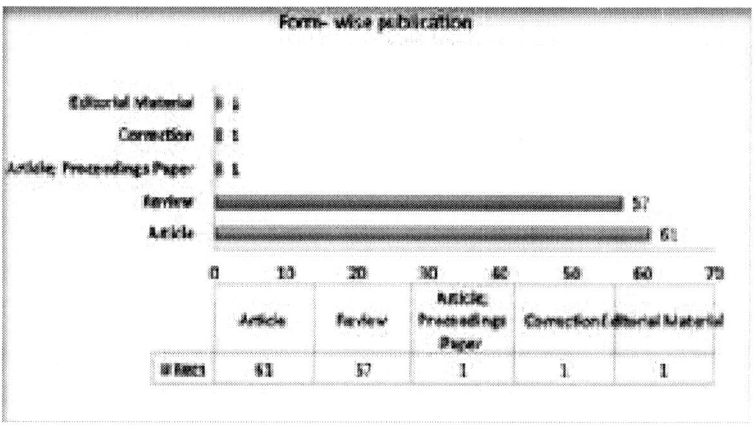

Fig. 3. Form-wise distribution

Year-wise growth of Literature

Table 2 and Figure 4-5 illustrate the growth rate of Indian literature performance and activity of researchers in terms of publication trends. In this regard, the publication productivity has increased two papers from 1994 to six papers in 2009 and in the year 2010 onwards, the growth level has started double digit i.e. 13 research papers (=10.7%) and suddenly the number has increased to 28 papers (=23.1%) and again decreased to 16 papers (=13.2%) in the year 2012 and in the year 2014 some minor growth rate is shown. The results bring out the growth analysis of phytochemistry in India is in the fluctuation trend. While we calculate in terms of citations, the huge number of citations (=436 citations) with 2 papers and the average citation per paper is 218 in the year 1997 and the least number of citations (=2 citations) with 2 papers and the average citation per paper is only one. The overall average citation is 103.28 during the study.

Table 2. Growth of Literature output-India

#	*PY*	*Recs*	*Percent*	*TC*	*CPP*
1	1994	2	1.7	2	1
2	1997	2	1.7	436	218
3	1999	1	0.8	4	4
4	2003	2	1.7	10	5
5	2004	3	2.5	53	17.67
6	2005	2	1.7	6	3
7	2006	1	0.8	159	159
8	2007	5	4.1	5	1
9	2009	6	5.0	203	33.83
10	2010	13	10.7	146	11.23
11	2011	28	23.1	241	8.61
12	2012	16	13.2	103	6.44
13	2013	18	14.9	52	2.89
14	2014	22	18.2	26	1.18

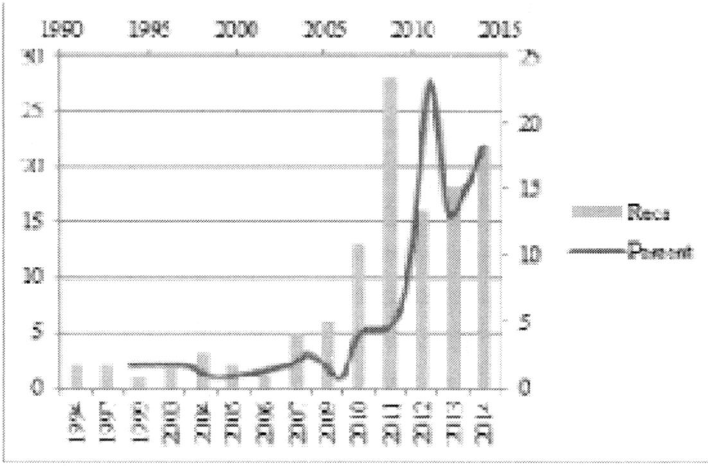

Fig. 4. Growth of Literature output-India

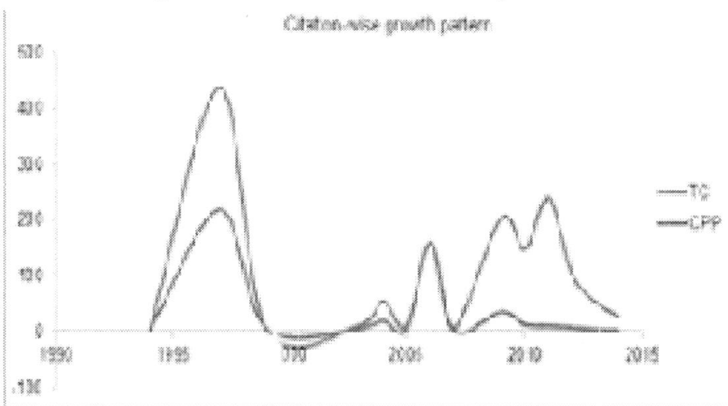

Fig. 5. Citation-wise growth pattern

Authorship pattern on Phytochemistry research

Table 3 depicts that authorship pattern of Phytochemistry in Indian research during the period of study. The maximum number of scientific publications (=469, 99.15%) were produced by the collaborative researchers and scientists. It identifies the majority of scholarly papers (=38, 114 authors) were written by three authors and has occupied in the first rank and followed by 24 research papers (=96 authors) were contributed by four authors and got by the second position. The third most productive research papers

(=20, 40 authors) were written by two authors and the least number of research articles (=1 paper, 8 authors) were contributed by eight authors and the average percentage of authors all over the papers is 8.33.

Table 3. Authorship pattern

Sl. No	*Pattern*	*Total Papers*	*Total authors*	*%age*	*Cumulative %age*
1	Single authors	4	4	3.31	3.31
2	Two Authors	20	40	16.53	19.84
3	Three Authors	38	114	31.40	51.24
4	Four Authors	24	96	19.84	71.08
5	Five Authors	19	95	15.70	86.78
6	Six Authors	7	42	5.79	92.57
7	Seven Authors	4	28	3.31	95.88
8	Eight Authors	1	8	0.82	96.7
9	Nine Authors	0	0	0	0
10	Ten Authors	0	0	0	0
11	Eleven Authors	2	22	1.65	98.35
12	Twelve Authors	2	24	1.65	100
	Total	121	473	100	

Single vs. Multi- authored research publications in Phytochemistry

To evaluate the authorship pattern in terms of single versus multi-authored literature outputs in Phytochemistry during the period of study, the degree of collaboration (DC) is used. The degree of collaboration (DC) is defined as the ratio of the number of collaborative research papers to the total number of research papers in the discipline during a certain period of time. This formula is suggested by Subramanyam (1983) is used and it is expressed as:

$$C = \frac{N_m}{N_m + N_s}$$

Where, C - denotes the degree of collaboration in a discipline; Nm- indicates the number of multi-authored research papers in the discipline published during a year; Ns- represents the number of single authored papers in the discipline published during the same year. Hence, it is observed based on the formula and it is found that the degree of collaboration in the Phytochemistry analysis is 0.99.

Table 4. Degree of collaboration (DC)

Sl. no	*Single Authors*	*%age*	*Multi-Authors*	*%age*	*Total Authors*	*Total %*	*DC*
1	4	0.85	469	99.15	473	100	0.99

Note : DC- Degree of Collaboration

FINDINGS AND CONCLUSION

The scientometric study is the best way to evaluate the scientific publications in any subject area. Phytochemistry is one of the thrust areas in the knowledge society. The major findings are that the highest number of research articles (=148, 11.6%) were published in 2014 throughout the world and the majority of Indian literature (=28, 23.1%) were produced in 201 1.The most of the documents are research articles (=50.4%) and placed in the first rank and based on the citations review articles are in the first rank (=1186 citations). The highest number of articles (=7, 5.8%) with 70 global citations published by the 'Father Muller Med College' and the same articles with 108 global citations and it is found that the word 'Review' has 36 record counts with 409 total citations and has placed in the first rank and followed by the word 'Phytochemistry' has 33 record counts with 655 citations and ranked in the second position.

REFERENCES

1. Aswathy, S and Gopikuttan, A. (2012) Journal of Spacecraft and Rockets: A Scientometric Analysis, SRELS Journal of Information Management, Vol. 49, No. 6, December 2012, Paper BQ. 671-682.

2 Mallik, Ajoy, and Nripendranath Mandal. (2013). Bibliometric analysis of global publication output and collaboration structure study in mircoRNA research, Scientometrics, 1-27.

3 Phytochemistry, http://www.yourdictionary.com/phytochemistry, visited on 24th July, 2016.

4 Phytochemistry,http://www.merriam-webster.com/dictionary/phytochemistry, visited on 24th July, 2016.

5 Phytochemistry,http://www.wordfind.com/word/phytochemistry/, visited on 24th July, 2016.

6 Phytochemistry,http://www.oxforddictionaries.com/definition/english/phytochemistry,visited on 6th August, 2016.

7 Shao, Hongfang, Qi Yu, Xiaoming Bo, and ZhiguangDuan (2013). Analysis of oncology research from 2001-2012: A scientometric perspective, Oncology reports 29(4), 1441-1452.

8 Velmurugan, C. and Radhakrishnan, N. (2015). Journal of Information Literacy: A Scientometric Profile, Journal of Information Sciences and Application, 3 (1), 1-9.

9 Velmurugan, C. and Radhakrishnan, N. (2015). Quantitative Analysis of Scientific Publications Output on Engineering Journal: A Scientometric Study, Journal of Information Sciences and Application, 3 (1), 19-30.

10 Velmurugan, C. and Radhakrishnan, N. (2015).Literature output of Supply Chain Management: A Scientometric approach, Journal of Organizational Behaviour, 3(2), 31-44.

11 Velmurugan, C. and Radhakrishnan, N. (2015). Collaborative Research and Authorship Pattern of Intellectual Property Rights,Journal of Information Management, 2(2), 77-87.

12 Velmurugan, C. & Radhakrishnan, N. (2015). Webology journal: a scientometric profile. International Journal of Information Dissemination and Technology (IJIDT), 5(2), 137-142.

13 Velmurugan, C. & Radhakrishnan, N. (2015).Scholarly Communications DESIDOC Journal of Library & Information Technology (DJLIT): a Scientometric approach International Journal of Library and Information Studies, 5 (3), 14-20.

14 Velmurugan, C. & Radhakrishnan, N. (2015). A Scientometric Analysis of Research Papers Published on Pharmacognosy as reflected in the Web of Science. Advances in Pharmacognosy and Phytomedicine, 1(1), 27-40.

15 Velmurugan, C. & Radhakrishnan, N. (2015). Scientometric observations of Authorship Trends and Collaborative Research

on DESIDOC Journal of Library and Information Technology, Collnet Journal of Scientometrics and Information Management, 9:2, 193-204, DOI: 10.1080/09737766.2015.1069957.

16 Velmurugan, C and Radhakrishnan, N. (2015). Research Productivity of Amylase in Microbiology in Indian Perspective: a Scientometric analysis, Microbial Production of Amylase in Bacillus Cereus Sp, Edited by Manimaran, D, Velmurugan, C and Elangovan, N, Dr, LAMBERT Academic Publishing (LAP), Germany, 128-143.

17 Velmurugan, C and Radhakrishnan, N. (2015). Authorship Trends and Collaborative research work on Library Herald: a Scientometric Analysis, Information Science and Digital Libraries edited by Somvir, S, International Research Publication House, Delhi, pp 173-186.

18 Velmurugan, C and Radhakrishnan, N. (2015). Literature output of Plagiarism: a Scientometric approach through Web of Science, Combating Plagiarism: a new role for Librarian edited by ManaswiniPatra and Sudhir Kumar Jena, S.K. Book Agency, New Delhi, pp 78-88.

19 Velmurugan, C. and Radhakrishnan, N. (2014). Research Analysis by means of Scientometric Techniques on Biotechnology, International Journal of Multidisciplinary Consortium (IJMC), 2 (1), 256-266.

20 Velmurugan, C. (2014). Research Trends in Journal of Intellectual Property Rights (JIPR): A Bibliometric Study,Library Philosophy and Practice (e-journal), Paper 1043. *http://digitalcommons.unl.edu/libphilprac/1043*

21 Velmurugan, C. (2014). Access Pattern of Online Journals among Library Users in Engineering College Central Libraries, Chennai, Tamilnadu, India: A Comparative Study, International Journal of Digital Library Services, 2014, 14-34.

22 Velmurugan, C. (2014). Research Trends in Indian Journal of Pure and Applied Physics (IJPAP) for the Year 2009 – 2012, Asian Review of Social Sciences, 3 (1), 2014, 24-28(ISSN: 2249 – 6319).

23 Velmurugan, C. (2014). Authorship Pattern and Collaborative Research Output of Indian Journal of Pure and Applied Physics (IJPAP), International Journal of Art & Humanity Science (IJAHS), 1 (2), (Sep-Oct), 37-41, e-ISSN: 2349-5235.

24 Velmurugan, C. and Radhakrishnan, N. (2014). Publication Research Trends on Technical Review Journal: A Scientometric Study, International Journal of Digital Library Services (IJDLS), 45-55.

25 Velmurugan, C (2014). Research Output with Special Reference to Authorship Pattern and Collaborative Research Work of the Journal of Intellectual Property Rights (JIPR) During 2007-2012,Journal of Information Technology and Library Science,2 (1), 1-8 (ISSN 2347 – 9760).

26 Velmurugan, C. (2013). Bibliometric analysis with special reference to Authorship Pattern and Collaborative Research Output of Annals of Library and Information Studies for the Year 2007 – 2012. International Journal of Digital Library Services, 3 (3), 2013, 13-21.

27 Yu, J.J., Wang, M.H. Xu, M.and Ho.Y.S. (2012). A bibliometric analysis of research papers published on photosynthesis: 19, 92-2009, Photosynthetica 50(1), 5-14.

20

A Bibliometric Study of Papers Published Indian Journal of Marketing : Year 2014

Shyamanta Boro
Assistant Librarian
University of Science & Technology, Meghalaya

ABSTRACT

The present paper is based on the citations of articles that are appeared in Indian Journal of Marketing is a double-blind peer-reviewed refereed monthly journal in the year 2014 from January to December where it covers 12 Issues. The study covers under the volume 44 from 1 to 12 Number of issues and total 55 articles are published having 1840 citations collectively. The citations are analyzed to find out the authorship pattern, distributions of different documents and to identify their institutions and locations, which are involved in contributing their own research. It is found that journals are used most frequently by the researchers of commerce and management. Results also reveal that a maximum number of articles is contributed by double authors 43 (78.19%) with a degree of collaboration 0.78.

Keywords : Bibliometric, Indian Journal of Marketing, Citations Analysis, Degree of collaboration, Quantitative analysis.

INTRODUCTION

Indian journal of marketing is a double blind peer reviewed refereed monthly journal in the field of marketing started in the year 1968 and it is the oldest and the only monthly journal of Marketing in India and completed 47 years of its research publications. The above cited title of the article the study throws bibliometric application of the Indian Journal of Marketing in the year 2014.

Bibliometrics is basically the combination of Latin and Greek word "Biblion" which means mathematical and statistical application. Thus the word "bibliometrics" means the measurement of books and it is known to all that it is the word "metrics" is suffixed to a field of activity, and then it indicates the application of mathematical and statistical methods to publications to that particular field. A bibliometrics analysis often used to study literature in a selected subject field where it is utilized quantitative analysis and statistics to describe patterns of publications.

DEFINITION

The term "Bibliometrics" has been first introduced by Alan Pritchard in the year 1969 and according to him the term "Bibliometrics" as the "Application of mathematical and statistical methods to books and other media of communication"

Bontiz has defined that "Bibliometrics is a methodological sub-discipline of library science; the complex of mathematical and statistical methods is used for analysis of the scientific and non-scientific document, library networks, indexing language, information systems, communication systems.

D.T. Hawkins defined it as "quantitative analysis of bibliographic features of body of literature"

According to Wikipedia, bibliometrics is a statistical analysis of written publications, such as books or articles. Bibliometric methods are frequently used in the field of library and information science, including scientometrics. For instance, bibliometrics are used to provide quantitative analysis of academic literature

LITERATURE REVIEW

Parveen Kumar (2013) in his study "A Bibliometric Study on Open Access Journals in Library Science Discipline in DOAJ" covered the issues brought out "Bulletin of the Medical Library Association" that was available before 1990 in the field of library and information science (LIS) and analyzed based on country, keywords, frequency, etc

Jayaprakash and B.U. Kannappanavar (2015) in their study "Citation Analysis of Doctoral Dissertations in Commerce Submitted to Goa University Goa: A Bibliometric Study" covered the issues of citations includes finding out authorship pattern, degree of collaboration, types of publications cited and chronological distribution of citations, guide wise distribution of the thesis, preparing list of ranked cited journals and authors in commerce thesis of Goa University

C. P. Salini, P. Nishy, R. S. Vishnumaya and S. Mini (2014) in their study "A Bibliometric Evaluation of Organic Chemistry Research in India" covered the countries, International Organizations and journals that cited the Indian contribution in the field.

Neera Bansal (2014) in his study "Prabandhan: Indian Journal of Management: A Citation Analysis" covered the citations and analyzed to find out authorship pattern, distribution of different document types and many more aspects

Zafrunnisha N and Pulla V Reddy (2009) in their study "Indian Journal of Marketing: A Bibliometric Study" covered authorship pattern, Bibliographic form, Subject, Language, Country and rank wise distribution of citations of articles appeared in IJM (XXX VI) published in the year 2006 i.e., January to December 2006

OBJECTIVES OF THE STUDY

- To measure the average number of references per article
- To find out the different forms of literature
- To find out the monthly authorship & Overall authorship pattern
- To find out Institutional affiliation of contributors
- To measure the space occupied by a article in determining the average length of the articles.
- To know the average number of Figures, Tables & Graphs appear in the article

SCOPE AND LIMITATIONS OF THE STUDY

The present study is limited to 1840 citations appended in the Indian Journal of Marketing that is already published in the year 2014 and study is limited to 12 issues.

METHODOLOGY

The present study is conducted with the aim of tracing the growth of journal output in the subject of marketing for the year 2014 (12 Issues) and for this study, data have been gathered manually from the Indian Journal of Marketing that is available in print format. Data have been collected from the 12 issues of monthly journal for the year 2014 and all data that are collected from these sources have been entered in Excel and analyzed in tabular and graphical forms

DATA ANALYSIS & DISCUSSION

The statistical and mathematical analysis of the "Indian Journal of Marketing" for the year 2014 (12 Issues) is applied the quite evaluative technique for making the successful result. It has been selected 12th issues for the year 2014 (Monthly). For evaluating and analyzing this literary information, there are applying of two types with source contribution i.e. articles and other is concerned with cited documents i.e. references article has been analyzed minutely without any particular consideration of subject field. It is fact that most of the articles are interdisciplinary in nature. The total number of article has been analyzed according to the given references respectively. Various statistical methods are applied in this analytical study of the journal article and to conclude this analytical study Bradford's Bibliometric laws are applied. All data are organized in the tabular form and organized data presented in the form of pie diagram and graph as far as possible.

Average Number of References per Article

Table – 1 represents the average number of reference per article month wise from January to December i.e. 12th Issues where highest average reference is shown in the month of January 61% with 4 Article and less average of reference is shown in the month of February 20.83% with 6 Article.

Table 1. Average Number of References per Article

Month	*No of Article*	*No of Reference*	*Average Citations Per Article %*
January	4	244	61
February	6	125	20.83
March	5	157	31.4
April	5	150	30
May	4	120	30
June	4	104	26
July	4	94	23.5
August	5	172	34.4
September	5	183	36.6
October	5	162	32.4
November	4	165	41.25
December	4	164	41
Total	55	1840	33.45

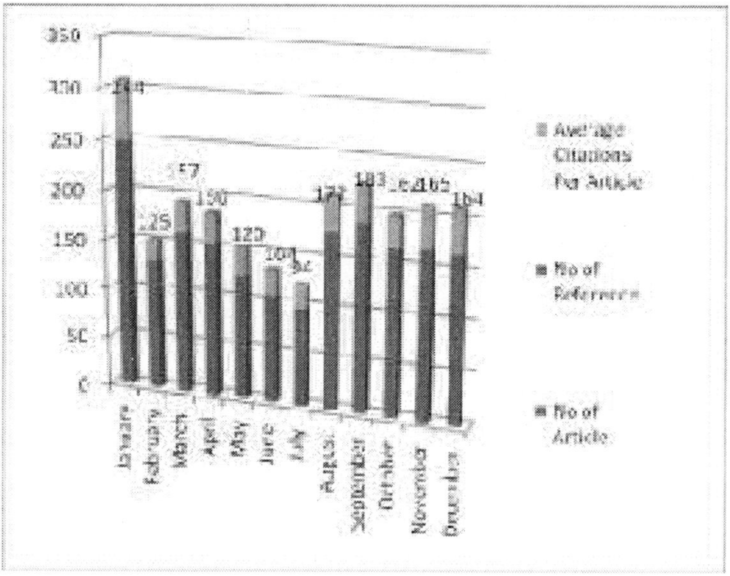

Fig. 1. Average Number of References per Article

Uses of different forms of literature

To find out the different forms of literature under 1840 citations in a tabular form Table 2 represents the highest citations of Journal is found with 1021 citations with Cumulative 55.4891% and Textbook citations found 570 with Cumulative 30.9782%, Web Cited reference 153 with Cumulative 8.3152%, Conference proceeding of 27 with Cumulative 1.4673%, Thesis 5 with Cumulative 0.2719% and the category of others is found 64 with Cumulative 3.4782%

Table 2. Uses of different forms of literature

Sl. No	*Form of document*	*No of Citations*	*Cumulative Citations*	*%*	*Cumulative %*
1	Journal	1021	1021	55.4891	55.4891
2	Book	570	1591	30.9782	30.9782
3	Web Reference	153	1744	8.3152	8.3152
4	Conference Proceeding	27	1771	1.4673	1.4673
5	Thesis	5	1776	0.2719	0.2719
6	Others	64	1840	3.4782	3.4782

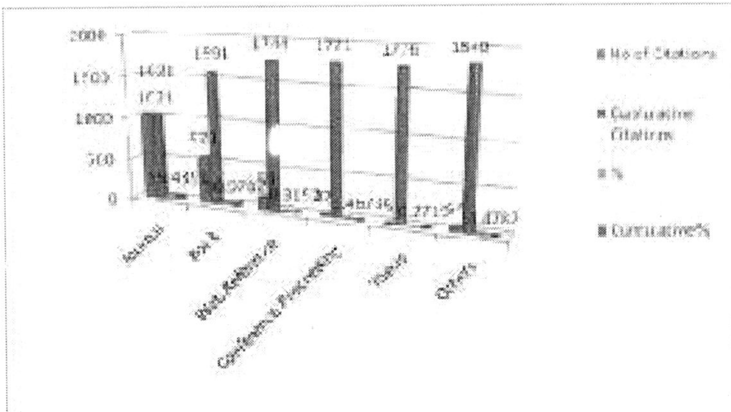

Fig. 2. Uses of different forms of literature

Monthly Authorship Pattern of Citing Articles

For showing the monthly authorship pattern of Indian Journal of Marketing from January to December 2014 (12 Issue) Table: 3. A - represents the highest monthly authorship pattern in the month of February 6th Author with 10.10% Cumulative and lowest authorship pattern is 4 with 7.28 % Cumulative.

Table: 3. B – represents overall authorship pattern where the study regarding the authorship pattern in the field of journal literature shows that majority of the article are double authored having 28 (50.91%) with (5.90%) Cumulative, Single authored articles having 12 (21.82%) with (2.18%) Cumulative, Triple authored articles 12 (21.82%) with (2.18%) cumulative. Four authored articles constitute 3 (5.46%) with (0.54%) cumulative.

Table 3. A–Monthly Authorship Pattern of Citing Articles

Sl No	*Month*	*Single Author*	*Two Author*	*Three Author*	*Four Author*	*Total Author*	*%*	*Cum. No Documents*	*Cum. %*
1	January	1	2	1	-	4	7.28	4	7.28
2	February	-	3	3	-	6	10.10	10	10.10
3	March	1	3	1	-	5	9.10	15	9.10
4	April	1	4	-	-	5	9.10	20	9.10
5	May	1	1	1	1	4	7.28	24	7.28

6	June	2	1	-	1	4	7.28	28	7.28
7	July	-	3	1	-	4	7.28	32	7.28
8	Augı st	-	4	-	1	5	9.10	37	9.10
9	September	3	1	1	-	5	9.10	42	9.10
10	October	2	-	3	-	5	9.10	47	9.10
11	November	1	2	1	-	4	7.28	51	7.28
12	December	-	4	-	-	4	7.28	55	7.28
	Total	**12**	**28**	**12**	**3**	**55**	**99.28**	**55**	**99.28**

Table 3. B – Overall Authorship Pattern

Authorship Pattern	*No. of Articles*	*Cumulative No. Article*	*%*	*Cumulative %*
One	12	12	21.82	2.18
Two	28	28	50.91	5.90
Three	12	12	21.82	2.18
Four	3	3	5.46	0.54
Total	**55**	**55**	**100**	**100**

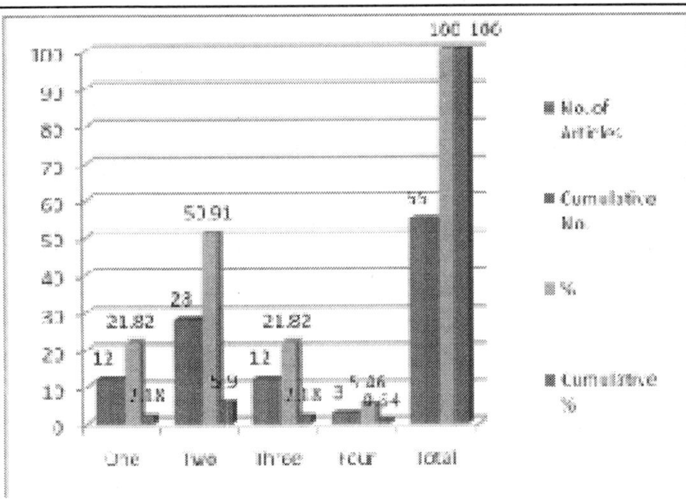

Fig. 3. Degree of collaboration of authorship pattern

Degree of Collaboration

The degree of collaboration is defined as the ratio of the number of collaborative research papers to the total number of research papers in the discipline during a certain period of time. The trend of collaborative research is measured by calculating degree of collaboration by using the formula stipulated by K Subramanyam

Formula is,

C = Nm/Nm+Ns

Where,

C = degree of collaboration in a discipline

Nm = Number of multi authored articles in a particular period

Ns = Number of single authored article in that period.

C is the degree of collaboration in a discipline. Nm is the number of multi-authored research papers in the discipline published during a year. Ns is the number of single authored research papers in the discipline published during a year.

Table 4 represents that the value of degree of collaboration with help of above mention formula by K Subramanyam and the result is 0.78

Table 4. Degree of Collaboration

Single Author	*%*	*Multi Author*	*%*	*Degree of Collaboration*	*Total Papers*
12	21.82	43	78.19	0.78	55

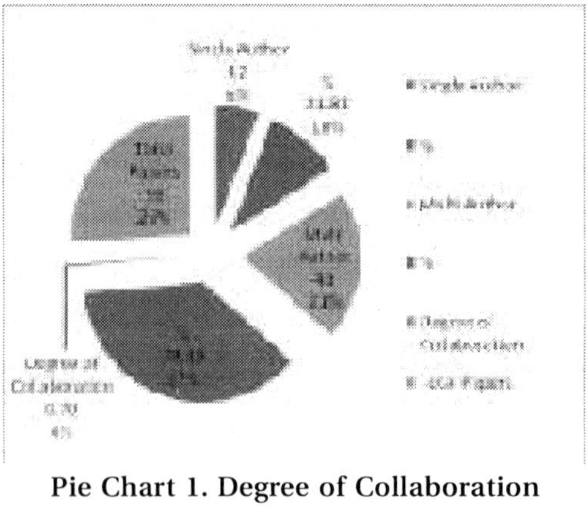

Pie Chart 1. Degree of Collaboration

Organization/Institution wise Contribution of Articles

To find out the organization or institutional belong to the contributors it was necessary to categories the institutions. The resultant analyzed revealed that the contributions belonged mainly four categories, they are like as University, College, Management/Technical Institutions and besides these three categories arranged one more category in the name of "Other" those institutional belonging author cannot be identified from the information available in the article are kept in that category.

Table 6 - reveals that majority of the contributor as well as author belonged to University 63 (54.311%) and Management & Technical Institute 39 (33.621%) and from College having 14 (12.069%) and where in the category of "Other" is not found.

Table 5. Organization wise Contribution of Articles

Sl No	*Type of Institutions*	*Total Contributors*	*%*
1	University	63	54.311
2	College	14	12.069
3	Management/ Technical Institute	39	33.621
4	Other	0	0
	Total	116	100

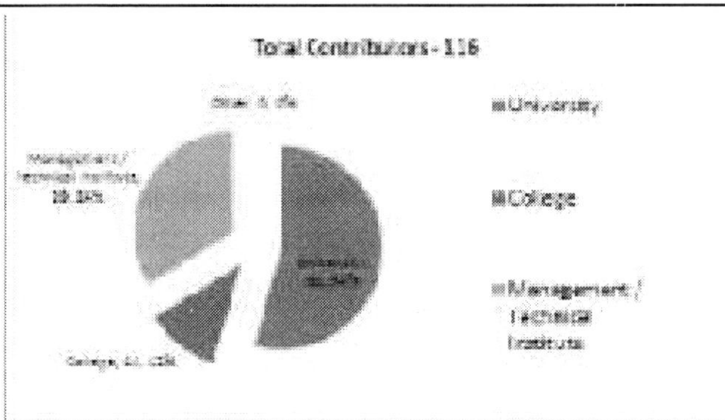

Pie Chart 2. Organization wise Contribution of Articles

Average Length of Articles

It is the measures of articles length where space is occupied by the article and it is necessary to find out the average length of the article by the contributor or author. To determine the average length of the article total number of pages covered by all articles of the corresponding issue is shown in Table 6 represents and all 55 articles cover 627 pages and the average length of article is 114.4 pages. The maximum length of articles is published in the in the month of June 55 with the average (13.75%) and in that month issue published 4 articles only.

Table 6. Average Length of Articles

Month	*No. of Article*	*No. of Pages*	*Average Pages Per Article*
January	4	51	12.75
February	6	55	9.16
March	5	46	9.2
April	5	46	9.2
May	4	51	12.75
June	4	55	13.75
July	4	53	13.25
August	5	59	11.8
September	5	54	10.8
October	5	53	10.6
November	4	54	13.5
December	4	50	12.5
Total	**55**	**627**	
Average Length of Article		**11.4**	

Distribution of Figures, Tables & Graphs

The researchers, as well as contributor of articles, are mostly preferred to use figures and tables and graphs for showing their findings and analysis. The presentation of figure and tables and graphs in a research article is the easier way to understand. Table 7 represents the figures, tables and graphs appended to articles during the period of study. It has found that total number of figures, tables and graphs are 91, 295 and 15 respectively with the average of 1.65 figures per article and 5.36 tables per article and 0.27 Graphs per articles. The maximum number of figures appear in the month of July with 17 (4.25 Average) followed by 12 in December average 3 whereas the maximum number of tables appeared in June 40 (10 average) followed by May 32 (8 Average) and the Graphs are appeared in only in the month of July with 15 (3.75 Average).

Table 7. Distribution of Figures and Tables & Graph

Month	*No. of Article*	*No. of Figures*	*Average No. of Figures*	*No. of Tables*	*Average No of Tables*	*Graph*	*Average No Graph*
January	4	10	2.5	11	2.75	-	-
February	6	11	1.83	35	5.83	-	-
March	5	2	0.4	16	3.2	-	-
April	5	1	0.2	18	3.6	-	-
May	4	2	0.5	32	8	-	-
June	4	9	2.25	40	10	-	-
July	4	17	4.25	26	6.5	15	3.75
August	5	4	0.8	31	6.2	-	-
September	5	5	1	19	3.8	-	-
October	5	7	1.4	26	5.2	-	-
November	4	11	2.75	22	5.5	-	-
December	4	12	3	19	4.75	-	-
Total	**55**	**91**		**295**		**15**	
Average	**1.65**	**5.36**	**0.27**				

CONCLUSION

Bibliometrics plays a significant role in the library and information managers as well as in their fields. It helps to know the trend of research by evaluation of research scholar's activity and also helps to evaluate a document. This study endeavoured to establish the relationship between statuses of the author's productivity. The findings obtained in this study showed that the productivity of a literature is directly related to his status in the department. Prestige, both personal and institutional is considered an important aspect of the productivity of a literature.

From the above study and analysis of data, we may derive the following findings

- Total number of reference is found 1840 in the 55 articles (12 Issued) where average is 33.45% and the highest number of references appeares in the month of January issued 244 in 4 articles with average is 61% and the lowest number of references appeares in the month of February 125 in 6 articles with average of 20.83% and February is the month where the highest number of articles appeared.
- From the 1840 number of references or citations it has analyzed in the table 2 and found the different forms of literature where highest number of citations found in the Journal category 1021 with Cumulative 55.4891% and Textbook citations found 570 with Cumulative 30.9782%, Web Cited reference 153 with Cumulative 8.3152%, Conference proceeding of 27 with Cumulative 1.4673%, Thesis 5 with Cumulative 0.2719% and the category of others is found 64 with Cumulative 3.4782%
- The authorship pattern of the selected journal is found in the month of February highest number of authorship pattern is found i.e. 6th Author with 10.10% Cumulative and lowest authorship pattern is 4 with 7.28 % Cumulative and to represents overall authorship pattern where the study regarding the authorship pattern majority of the articles are double authored having 28 (50.91%) with (5.90%) Cumulative, Single authored articles having 12 (21.82%) with (2.18%) Cumulative, Triple authored articles 12 (21.82%) with (2.18%) cumulative. Four authored articles constitute

3 (5.46%) with (0.54%) cumulative.

- The degree of collaboration is measured with the help of formula by K Subramanyam and the result is 0.78
- The majority of the contributor of journal literature, as well as author, belonged to University 63 (54.311%) and Management & Technical Institute 39 (33.621%) and from College having 14 (12.069%) and wherein the category of "Other" is not found
- The overall lengths of the articles appeared in the journal found 55 articles and cover 627 pages and the average length of the article is 114.4 pages. The maximum length of articles is published in the in the month of June 55 with an average (13.75%) and in that month issue published 4 articles only.
- It has found that the highest number of figures, tables and graphs represents 91, 295 and 15 respectively with the average of 1.65 figures per article and 5.36 tables per article and 0.27 Graphs per articles. The maximum number of figures appear in the month of July with 17 (4.25 Average) followed by 12 in December average 3 whereas the maximum number of tables appeared in June 40 (10 average) followed by May 32 (8 Average) and the Graphs are appeared in only in the month of July with 15 (3.75 Average)

REFERENCES

1. Bansal, N. (2014). Prabandhan: Indian Journal of Management: A Citation Analysis. Global Journal For Research Analysis, Vol. 3 (1), pp.19 – 21.
2. Barman, R. K. (1998). A Bibliometric study. G.U. Journal of Arts 1975 - 1955. Two decades of G.U. Journal of Arts, Vol. 39, pp.1-5.
3. Bibliometrics: an overview : University of Leeds http://www.ndlr.ie/myri/ (22/08/2015)
4. Boro, S. (2010). Bibliometric Study of Bodo Literature from 2005 to 2009. Department of Library and Information Science, Gauhati University (Dissertation Unpublished).

5. Dxit. S and Katare V. V. (2007). A Biblimetric Analysis of the Journal of Indian Society for Cotton Improvement 1995-2004. Annals of Library & Information Studies, Vol 54. Pp. 119-123.

6. Garg, C. C. and Dutta B. (1992). Bibliometrics of agriculture research in india. ILLAD Quarterly Bulletin, Vol.34 (5), pp.133-139

7. Gomez, M. (2002). A Bibliometric Study to Manage a Journal Collection in An Astronomical Library: Some Results. Library and Information Services in Astronomy, Vol. IV.

8. Gupta, S.P (1997). Statistical Method. New Delhi: Sultan Chand and Sons

9. Hawkins, D. T. (2001). Bibliometrics of Electronic Journals in Information Science. Information Research, Vol. 7(1)

10. http://ijsr.indianjournals.com/ijor.aspx?target=ijor:pjolis&volume=3&issue=4&article=004 (05/08/2015)

11. http://www.ijodls.in/uploads/3/6/0/3/3603729/vol-5,_issue-2.160-177.pdf (18/08/2015)

12. http://www.indianjournalofmarketing.com/index.html (22/08/2015)

13. http://www.publishingindia.com/ijils/52/a-bibliometric-study-on-open-access (22/08/2015)

14. https://en.wikipedia.org/wiki/Bibliometrics (20.08.2015)

15. Kabir, H. (2000). World Literature on Bibliometrics: Authorship And Growth Patterns. ILA Bulletin, Vol. 28 (3-4), Pp.87-94

16. Keshava, V.P and Hittalamani (2008). Papers in Select Sociology Journals (1999-2004): A Bibliometric Analysis. Journal of Information Studies, Vol.14 (1), pp. 56-58.

17. Pritchard, A (1969). Statistical Bibliography of Bibliometrics. Jr. of Doc. Vol.25 (4), pp.348-349

18. Sen, B.K (1988). Bibliometrics in India: A Review. ILA Bulletin. Vol. 26(4), pp.24-27.

19. Salini, C. P., Nishy, P., Vishnumaya, R.S. and Mini, S. (2014). A Bibliometric Evaluation of Organic Chemistry research In India. Annals of Library & Information Studies, Vol. 61 Pp.332-342

20. Swain, D. K. (2014). Journal Bibliometric Analysis: A Case Study on Quality Assurance in Education. Indian Streams Research Journal, Vol.4 (4) pp. 1-14 http://www.isrj.net

21

Growth of Literature on Geophysics : A Scientometric Profile

R. Santha kumar
Young Professional II
ICAR - Central Institute of Brackishwater Aquaculture,
#75, Santhome High Road, R A Puram,
Chennai - 600 028, Tamil Nadu

ABSTRACT

The present chapter is aimed at analyzing the global publication trends in geophysics using Web of Science database for the period 2000-2015. A total of 3745 publications were published in the field and the average number of publications published per year was 234.06. The highest number of publications 328 was published in 2015 and the lowest number of publications 139 in 2000. Relative Growth Rate is decreasing throughout the study period and corresponding Doubling time is increasing. Average RGR is 0.22 and corresponding Doubling time is 4.62. The web of science database allows us to refine the results in terms of publication years, top authors, top countries, top organizations, most influential source titles, language and subjects.

Keywords : Geophysics, scientometric analysis, RGR and DT

INTRODUCTION

Geophysics is a non-destructive and non-invasive Earth Science that uses the very latest science and technology in instrumentation, data acquisition and advanced computer modelling and interpretation in subsurface exploration. Geophysics is an interdisciplinary physical science concerned with the nature of the earth and its environment and as such seeks to apply the knowledge and techniques of physics, mathematics and chemistry to understand the structure and dynamic behaviour of the earth and its environment. Geophysics is applied to societal needs, such as mineral resources, mitigation of natural hazards and environmental protection, Geophysical survey data are used to analyze potential petroleum reservoirs and mineral deposits, locate groundwater, find archaeological relics, determine the thickness of glaciers and soils, and assess sites for environmental remediation.

The use of geophysical technology is not limited to the resources industry. It's also used in many other areas of scientific research and exploration. In Archaeology, geophysics is used to uncover the remains of buried cities, walls, ancient watercourses and graves among other things. Ground penetrating radar and resistivity profiling are two of the many methods used here. In Oceanography and Atmospherics geophysics is used to analyse the structure and motion of the atmosphere and oceans. Today, geophysical methods are used extensively in subsurface exploration because they produce fast and accurate results and are, more importantly, non-destructive and non-invasive. Therefore, the present study has been undertaken in order to know the growth and development of publications in the field of geophysics research as indexed in web of science database.

OBJECTIVES OF THE STUDY

The objective of the study was to perform a scientometric analysis of all geophysics publications in the world. The parameters studied include:

- Annual growth rate, compound growth rate of publications
- Highly prolific authors
- Highly productive countries
- Highly productive institutes
- Most preferred source titles for publication
- Language-wise distribution of publications
- High productive subject areas

METHODOLOGY

The data for the present study was retrieved from Web of Science database which is published by Thomson Reuters. This is one of the largest-established and best known bibliographic databases for science, social science, arts and humanities and it covers more than 90 million records referencing 256 disciplines of journals, conference materials and technical reports dating from 1900. A total of 3745 records were downloaded from the Web of Science database during 2000-2015 and analysed by using the spreadsheet application as per the objectives of the study.

DATA ANALYSIS AND INTERPRETATIONS

Growth of publications

Table 1 provides the AGR and CAGR of the number of documents for period 2000 to 2015.

$$AGR = \frac{\text{End Value} - \text{First Value}}{\text{First Value}} \times 100$$

Table 1. AGR and CAGR of Publications

Year	*No. of publications*	*Cumulative total*	*Annual growth rate (AGR)*	*CAGR*
2000	139	139	-	-
2001	165	304	118.70	0.84
2002	168	472	55.26	0.68

2003	208	680	44.07	0.48
2004	208	888	30.59	0.44
2005	195	1083	21.96	0.41
2006	235	1318	21.70	0.32
2007	232	1550	17.60	0.30
2008	221	1771	14.26	0.28
2009	243	2014	13.72	0.26
2010	238	2252	11.82	0.25
2011	228	2480	10.12	0.24
2012	311	2791	12.54	0.19
2013	300	3091	10.75	0.18
2014	326	3417	10.55	0.18
2015	328	3745	9.60	0.16

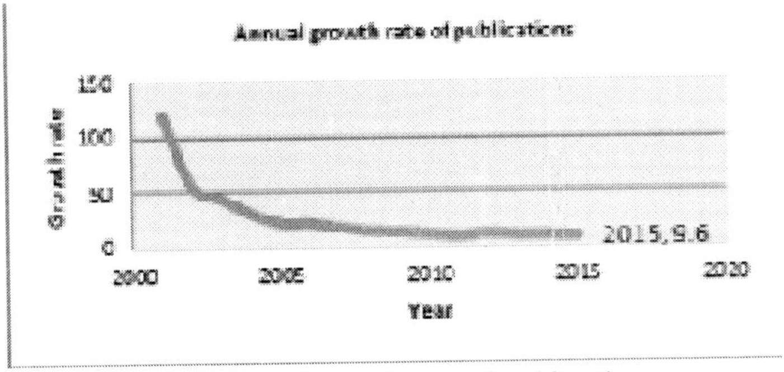

Fig. 1. Annual growth rate of publications

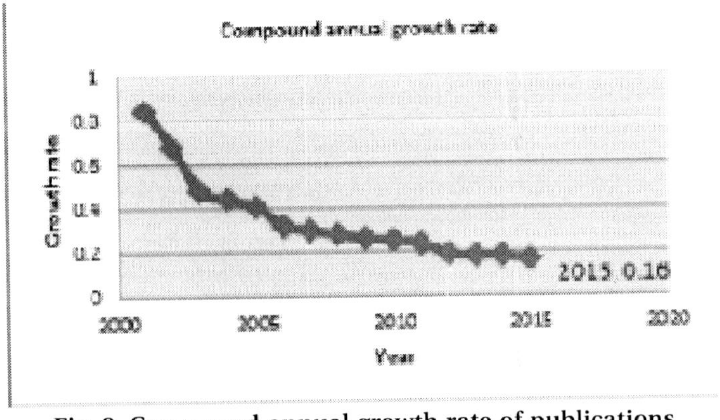

Fig. 2. Compound annual growth rate of publications

The table 1 and figure 1 reveal that during the period of 2000 to 2015, a total of 3,745 publications were published on geophysics research. The highest number of publications is 328 was published in 2015. The lowest publications of 139 are published in 2000. The average number of publications published per year was 234.06. The table 1 also shows that the annual growth rate of the total publications calculated year wise. AGR reveals that it has decreased from 118.70 in 2001 to 9.60 in 2015. There is a decreasing trend in the growth rate in the study period.

The compound annual growth rates of the publications are gradually decreased from 0.84 in 2001 to 0.16 in 2015 as seen in Table 1. This indicates that the compound annual growth rate is in a downward trend.

Relative Growth Rate (RGR) and Doubling Time

The Relative Growth Rate (RGR) is the increase in the number of articles or pages per unit of time. This definition derived from the definition of relative growth rates in the study of growth analysis in the field of geophysics. The mean relative growth rate (R) over the specific period of the interval can be calculated from the following equation.

Relative Growth Rate (RGR)

$$1 - 2R = \text{Log } W_2 - \text{Log } W_1 / T_2 - T_1$$

Whereas

- 1-2 R- mean relative growth rate over the specific period of interval
- Loge W_1 - log of initial number of articles
- Loge W_2 - log of final number of articles after a specific period of interval
- T_2-T_1- the unit difference between the initial time and the final time
- The year can be taken here as the unit of time.
- Doubling Time (DT) = 0.693/R

Table 2. Relative growth rate (RGR) and Doubling time (DT) of publications

Year	*No. of Publications*	*Cumulative Total*	*W1*	*W2*	*RGR*	*DT*
2000	139	139	-	4.93	-	-
2001	165	304	4.93	5.72	0.79	0.88
2002	168	472	5.72	6.16	0.44	1.56
2003	208	680	6.16	6.52	0.36	1.93
2004	208	888	6.52	6.79	0.27	2.57
2005	195	1083	6.79	6.99	0.20	3.47
2006	235	1318	6.99	7.18	0.19	3.65
2007	232	1550	7.18	7.35	0.17	4.08
2008	221	1771	7.35	7.48	0.13	5.33
2009	243	2014	7.48	7.61	0.13	5.33
2010	238	2252	7.61	7.72	0.11	6.30
2011	228	2480	7.72	7.82	0.10	6.93
2012	311	2791	7.82	7.93	0.11	6.30
2013	300	3091	7.93	8.04	0.11	6.30
2014	326	3417	8.04	8.14	0.10	6.93
2015	328	3745	8.14	8.23	0.09	7.7

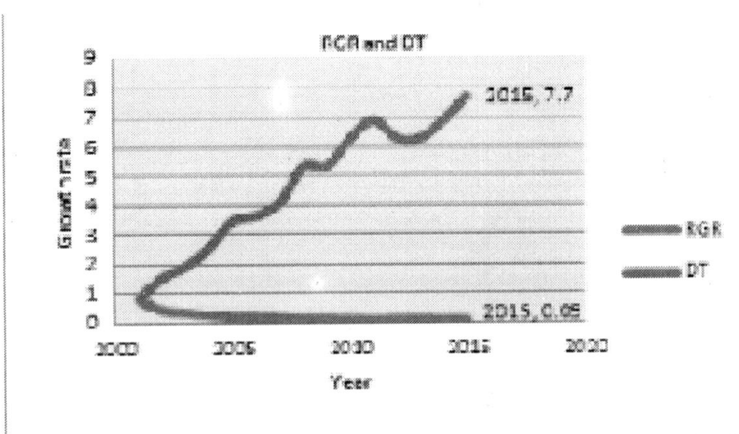

Fig. 3. Relative growth rate for research output

The year wise RGR is found to be in the range of 0.79 to 0.09. Year wise calculation of RGR reveals that it has gradually decreased from 2001 to 2015. The highest value 0.79 corresponds to the year 2001, whereas the lowest value 0.09 for the year 2015.

Doubling time too has a trend similar to that of RGR. Its ranges are from 0.88 to 7.70 (figure 3). A year-wise increase is seen during the study period.

Trend Analysis – Method of Least Squares

The least square method is the best method for obtaining the trend values which is often used to analyse the counting trends, population growth etc. The line of the best fit is a line from which the sum of the deviations of various points on its either side is zero. Further, the sum of the squares of these deviations would be the least as compared to the sum of squares of the deviations obtained by using other lines.

The straight line trend has an equation of the type:

$$Y = a + bX,$$

Where, Y represents the estimated values of the trend, X represents the deviations in the time period; 'a' and 'b' are constants.

The values of two constants 'a' and 'b' are estimated by solving the following two normal equations.

$$\Sigma Y = Na + b\Sigma X$$

$$\Sigma XY = a\ \Sigma X + b\Sigma X2$$

Where N represents number of years for which data is given.

The variable X can be measured from any point of time as the origin. To make calculation simpler, it is better to take the mid-point of time as the origin because the negative values of first half of the time series will equalize the positive values in the second half of the series which symbolically gives $\Sigma X = 0$.

When ΣX = 0, the two normal equations for finding the constants 'a' and 'b' will be

$$\Sigma Y = Na \Rightarrow a = \frac{\Sigma Y}{N} = Y$$

$$\Sigma XY = b\Sigma X2 \Rightarrow b =$$

This provides that the constant 'a' is simply equal to the mean of Y values and the constant 'b' gives the rate of change. The constant 'a' refers to the Y intercept, i.e. the difference between the point of origin and the point where the trend line touches the Y axis. The constant 'b' refers to the slope of the line which indicates the change in Y for each unit change in X.

Table 3. Computation of Straight Line Trend by the Least Squares Method

Year	*No. of Publications Actual (Y)*	*Deviation*	*Multiply (X)*	*XY*	X^2	*Trend value*
2000	139	-7.5	-15	-2085	225	149
2001	165	-6.5	-13	-2145	169	161
2002	168	-5.5	-11	-1848	121	172
2003	208	-4.5	-9	-1872	81	183
2004	208	-3.5	-7	-1456	49	195
2005	195	-2.5	-5	-975	25	206
2006	235	-1.5	-3	-705	9	217
2007	232	-0.5	-1	-232	1	228
2008	221	1	1	221	1	240
2009	243	1.5	3	729	9	251
2010	238	2.5	5	1190	25	262
2011	228	3.5	7	1596	49	274
2012	311	4.5	9	2799	81	285
2013	300	5.5	11	3300	121	296
2014	326	6.5	13	4238	169	307
2015	328	7.5	15	4920	225	319

2016	17			330
2017	19			341
2018	21			353
2019	23			364
2020	25			375
2021	27			386
2022	29			398
2023	31			409
2024	33			420
2025	35			431
		7675	1360	7552

The equation of the straight line trend is Y = a + bX

Since $\Sigma X=0$, therefore

$$a = \frac{\Sigma Y}{N} = \quad = 374.5$$

$$b = \frac{\Sigma XY}{\Sigma X^2} = \frac{7675}{1360} = 5.64$$

Substituting the value of 'a' and 'b' in the straight line of the trend,

$Y = a + bX \Rightarrow Y = 234.06 + 5.64 \times X$

Estimate of 2025 will be calculated on the basis of

$X = 35$

$Y2025 = 234.06 + 5.64 \times 35 = 431$

With the use of the trend analysis, the trend values are calculated up to 2025. The trend line and actual line are presented in figure 4. And, it is seen from the table that the actual trend was standard in the year 2000 since then there is an upward trend up to the end of the year 2025. During the study period, there is a fluctuations trend in the prediction line. From this, it can be interpreted that the fluctuations in the actual line reflect in the trend line also.

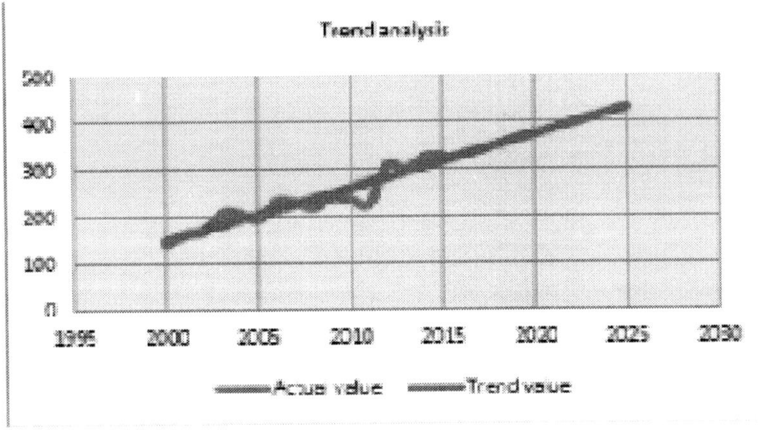

Fig. 4. Trend of the geophysics literature

Identification of most prolific authors

Table 4. Identification of most prolific authors

Rank	*Author*	*No. of publications*	*Percentage*
1	Anonymous	17	0.45%
2	Pringle, J K	14	0.37%
3	Grott, M	13	0.32%
4	Crampin, S	12	0.32%
5	Liu, L B	12	0.32%
6	Revil, A	12	0.32%
7	Zuber, M T	12	0.32%
8	Kerr, R A	10	0.27%
9	Slater, L	10	0.27%
10	Wan, W X	10	0.27%

The authors having 10 or more publications during 2000-2015 are shown in Table 4. Anonymous is the most productive author with 17 (0.45%) publications followed by Pringle, J K with 14 (0.37%) publications, Grott, M with 13 (0.32%) publications, Crampin, S with 12 (0.32%) publications, Liu, L B with 12 (0.32%) publications, Revil, A with 12 (0.32%) publications and Zuber, M T with 12 (0.32%) publications, respectively. And a total of 10,794 authors are contributed entire research output of the period under study.

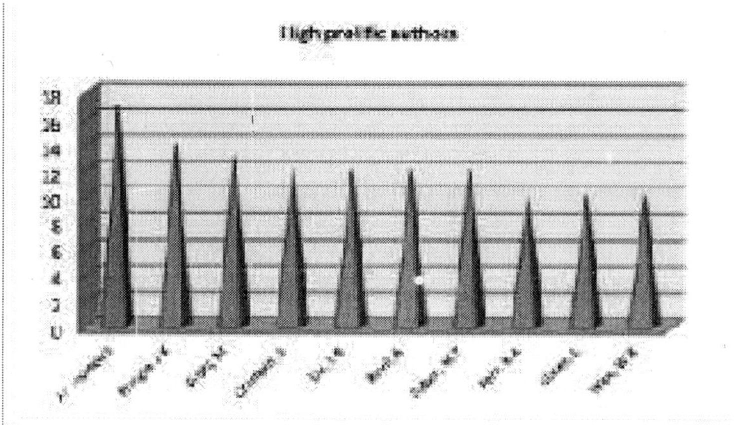

Fig. 5. High prolific authors

Highly productive institutes

Table 5. Highly productive institutes

Rank	*Institutions*	*Country*	*No. of Publications*
1	Russian Academy of Sciences	Russia	119 (3.18%)
2	Chinese Academy of Sciences	China	96 (2.56%)
3	California Institute of Technology	USA	78 (2.08%)
4	US Geological Survey	USA	54 (1.44%)
5	Centre National de la Recherché Scientifique	France	50 (1.34%)
6	Woods Hole Oceanographic Institution	USA	49 (1.31%)
7	China University of Geosciences	USA	42 (1.12%)
8	Colorado School of Mines	USA	41 (1.10%)
9	British Geological Survey	UK	40 (1.07%)
10	University of California, Berkeley	USA	39 (1.04%)

A total of 2940 institutions are contributed entire research output of the study. The scientometric profile of top 10 institutions is presented in table 5. Among these top 10 institutions, 6 are from the USA and each 1 from Russia, China, France and UK. Findings revealed that Russian

Academy of Sciences, Russia with 119 (3.18%) publications is the most productive institutions in the field of geophysics research followed by Chinese Academy of Science, China with 96 (2.56%) publications, California Institute of Technology, USA with 78 (2.08%) publications, US Geological Survey, USA with 54 (1.44%) publications, Centre National de la Recherché Scientifique, France with 50 (1.34%) publications, Woods Hole Oceanographic Institution, USA with 49 (1.31%) publications, China University of Geosciences, USA with 42 (1.12%) publications, Colorado School of Mines, USA with 41 (1.10%) publications and British Geological Survey, UK with 40 (1.07%) publications.

Highly productive countries

Table 6. Highly productive countries

Rank	*Country*	*Total Publications (%)*
1.	USA	1164 (31.08%)
2.	France	396 (10.57%)
3.	Germany	319 (8.52%)
4.	China	301 (8.04%)
5.	England	289 (7.72%)
6.	Italy	287 (7.66%)
7.	Canada	226 (6.04%)
8.	Australia	216 (5.77%)
9.	Russia	187 (4.99%)
10.	Japan	127 (3.39%)
11.	Spain	117 (3.12%)
12.	India	105 (2.80%)
13.	Switzerland	100 (2.67%)

In all, there were 101 countries involved in the research in geophysics; however, USA topped the list with highest share (31.08%) of publications. France ranked second with 10.57% share of publications followed by Germany 8.52% share of publications, China with 8.04% share of publications, England with 7.72% share of publications, Italy with 7.66%

share of publications, Canada with 6.04% share of publications, Australia with 5.77% share of publications, Russia with 4.99% share of publications and the remaining countries are publishing less than 4% of the research output in this study period. The publication share of highly productive countries (≥100 publications) on geophysics is given in Table 6.

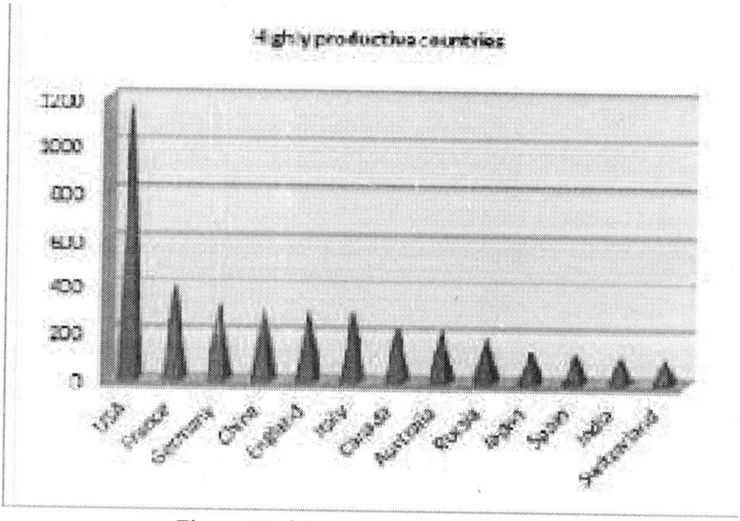

Fig. 6. Highly productive countries

Language wise distributions

Table 7. Language wise distributions

Rank	*Language*	*No. of Publications*
1	English	3603 (96.21%)
2	Chinese	84 (2.24%)
3	French	23 (0.61%)
4	Russian	11 (0.29%)
5	German	6 (0.16%)
6	Spanish	5 (0.13%)
7	Portuguese	4 (0.11%)
8	Polish	3 (0.08%)
9	Slovak	2 (0.05%)

10	Swedish	2 (0.05%)
11	Croatian	1 (0.03%)
12	Italian	1 (0.03%)
13	Slovenian	1 (0.03%)

Publications on geophysics are spread over 13 languages. The study reveals that the maximum number of publications have been published in English language with 3603 (96.21%) publications, followed by Chinese language with 84 (2.24%) publications, French language ranks third position with 23 (0.61%) publications, Russian language with 11 (0.29%) publications, German language with 6 (0.16%) publications, Spanish language with 5 (0.13%) publications and Portuguese with 4 (0.11%) publications. And the remaining languages such as Polish, Slovak, Swedish and other languages are constituted in negligible percentage. The English language superiority was found in every year in total productivity on the subject during the study period.

Most preferred source titles

Table 8. Source Title of Publications

Rank	*Source title*	*No. of publications*	*%age*	*Impact factor*
1.	Geochemistry geophysics geosystems	269	7.18%	5.6
2.	Geophysics	163	4.35%	1.759
3.	ICARUS	130	3.47%	3.161
4.	Journal of applied geophysics	109	2.91%	1.355
5.	Chinese journal of geophysics Chinese edition	68	1.81%	0.703
6.	Geophysical journal international	68	1.81%	2.420
7.	Science	54	1.44%	34.661
8.	Geophysical prospecting	47	1.26%	1.835
9.	Computers geosciences	46	1.23%	2.474
10.	Annals of geophysics	44	1.18%	1.037

The publication share of most productive source titles (≥40 publications) on geophysics is given in Table 8. The scientific literature on geophysics is spread over 848 different source journals. It reveals that Geochemistry geophysics geosystems the list with the highest number of publications 269 (7.18%) and the impact factor is 5.6, followed by Geophysics with a share of 163 (4.35%) publications and the impact factor is 1.759. ICARUS occupies the third position with 130 (3.47%) publications and the impact factor is 3.161. The fourth highest source title is Journal of applied geophysics with 109 (2.91%) publications and the impact factor is 1.355, Chinese journal of geophysics Chinese edition with 68 (1.81%) publications and the impact factor is 0.703 and Geophysical journal international with 68 (1.81%) publications and the impact factor is 2.420.

High productivity subject areas

Table 9. High productivity subject areas

Rank	*Subject*	*No. of Articles*	*Percentage*
1	Geochemistry geophysics	1212	32.36%
2	Geology	1108	29.59%
3	Engineering	393	10.49
4	Astronomy astrophysics	311	8.30
5	Physics	310	8.28%
6	Meteorology atmospheric sciences	188	5.02%
7	Water resources	179	4.78%
8	Environmental sciences ecology	155	4.14%
9	Mining mineral processing	154	4.11%
10	Mathematics	153	4.09%

Table 9 shows high productivity subjects which are contributing more than 150 articles. It is found that Geochemistry geophysics has the highest number of articles with 1212 (32.36%) followed by Geology contributing 1108 (29.59%) articles. Engineering occupies the third position with 393 (10.49%) articles. The fourth highest articles belonged to the subject Astronomy astrophysics with 311 (8.30%), Physics with 310 (8.28%) and Meteorology atmospheric sciences with 188 (5.02%) articles respectively.

CONCLUSION

The present chapter attempted to highlight the growth and development of research production in geophysics. A total of 3745 publications were published during 2000-2015 and the average number of publications per year was 234.06. There was a fluctuations trend in the growth of publications during the study period. The USA topped the list with highest share (31.08%) of publications. France ranked second with 10.57% share of publications followed by Germany 8.52% share of publications and China with 8.04% share of publications. Publications on geophysics are spread over 13 languages. Russian Academy of Sciences, Russia topped the list with 119 (3.18%) publications followed by Chinese Academy of Science, China with 96 (2.56%) publications and California Institute of Technology, USA with 78 (2.08%) publications. The scientific literature on geophysics is spread over 848 different source journals. The most preference journals for publications were Geochemistry geophysics geosystems with 269 publications followed by Geophysics with 788 publications and Bioinformatics with 596 publications.

REFERENCES

1. Stanhill, G. (2001). The growth of climate change science: a scientometric study, Climatic Change, Vol. 48, No. 2-3, pp. 515-524.
2. Garg, K.C. (2001). Scientometrics of laser research in India and China, 8th International Conference on Scientometrics and Informetrics. Proceedings - ISSI-2001, Vol. 1, Pt. 1, pp. 167-177
3. Santha kumar R. Publications Trends in Nuclear Physics: A Global Perspective" (2016). Library Philosophy and Practice (e-journal). Paper 1361. http://digitalcommons.unl.edu/libphilprac/1361
4. Santha kumar R. Research Trends in Medical Physics: A Global Perspective" (2016). Library Philosophy and Practice (e-journal). Paper 1362. http://digitalcommons.unl.edu/libphilprac/1362

5. Santha kumar R and Kaliyaperumal K. A Scientometric Analysis of Mobile Technology Publications, Scientometrics, 2015, 105 (2): 921-939

6. Santha Kumar, R. & Kaliyaperumal, K. Scientometric Analysis of Global Publication Output in Mobile Technology: A Scientometric Study, DESIDOC Journal of Library and Information Technology, 2015, 35(4): 287-292

7. Santha kumar R and Kaliyaperumal K. Scientometric Analysis with Special Reference to Mobile Technology Publications for the Year 2003 – 2013, International Journal of Information Library & Society, 2015, 4 (1): 1-8

8. Santha kumar R and Kaliyaperumal K. Mapping of Mobile Technology Publications: A Scientometric Approach, DESIDOC Journal of Library and Information Technology, 2014, 34(4): 298-303

9. https://en.wikipedia.org/wiki/Geophysics

22

Mapping of Research Productivity in Madurai Kamaraj University: A Scientometric Study

R. Senthilkumar
Librarian (SG) & Head (Research)
Department of Library and Information Science,
Kongunadu Arts & Science College (Autonomous),
Coimbatore-641 029, Tamil Nadu

G. Ulaganathan
Research Scholar Ph.D (PT),
Kongunadu Arts & Science College (Autonomous),
Coimbatore - 641 029. & Librarian,
Dr. SNS. Rajalakshmi College of Arts &
Science (Autonomous), Coimbatore-641 049, Tamil Nadu

ABSTRACT

This paper discusses the published research articles and its citation available in the Indian Citation Index by the authors from Madurai Kamaraj University. The relevant data are collected from Indian Citation Index and it was analyzed. It shows among the published 414 articles, the maximum of 45(10.87%) articles published in 2008&2011 and minimum of 23(5.56%) articles published in 2004. The Citations study shows that the maximum of 50(25.38%) citations in 2005 and minimum number of citations 4(2.03%) in 2015.

Keywords : Mapping, Research Productivity ICI, Year wise Distribution, Citation Analysis, Madurai Kamaraj University, Scientometric.

INTRODUCTION

The true barometer of assessing the quality and quantity of a journal is the Citation Index. While discussing citation, one needs to understand the citation. Simply, when another refers other works in his/her article, we call the article referred is cited. In other words, the citation is called as the previous work which is referred in the present work. The quality of a given work can rightly be adjudged through the number of citations that it gets. Therefore, a certain piece of article or research paper is carrying more number of citations get more impact than the work carrying fewer citations. Therefore, we always refer to some indexing and abstracting databases like Scopus, Web of Science, or even Google Scholars to know the impact of a journal, a particular article or a particular author. Indian Citation Index which was initiated by Diva Enterprises is just an indexing and abstracting database.

REVIEW OF LITERATURE

Nicholas and Ritchie (1978)[1] view that, "study of bibliometrics concept provides information, knowledge and how it is communicated". Moreover, bibliometrics studies are normally employed to evaluate the academic research output, the quality of the journal, impact and influence of articles, authors, and assorted parameters. Though there has been the substantial growth of literature on bibliometrics studies during the last decade, the authors focus on some of the pertinent literature that relate to the present study. Potter (1981)[2] defines bibliometric analysis as "the calculation and study of the research publication patterns of all types of written communication and their authorship nature". In a most interesting study Mooghali (2011)[3]et al analyzed records of three premiere indexes known as, "SSCI", "SCI", and "AHCI", and it is projected in the field of "scientometrics" evolved between 1980 to 2009. The pattern of growth of literature in the field of Nanoscience during 1990 to 2009 was reported by Karpagam et al. (2011)[4]. In the similar vein, Abramo (2011)[5] exercised bibliometric techniques on some national level research assessment. Lapon-Kandeishein and Prebor (2011)[6] bibliographical research on Hebrew printing also needs mention. In the similar light bibliometric studies by veterans like Krampen, Eye and Schui (2011)[7], Kumar Suchetan(2012)[8] and others also presented findings from different directions. Dhanavandan and Tamizhchelvan (2014)[9] studied citations and research productivity of south Tamil Nadu universities from 2009 to 2013 based on Indian Citation Index (ICI).

METHODOLOGY

This study aims to discuss the analysis of the citation index of the research output by faculty members of Madurai Kamaraj University. The relevant sources and data are collected from Indian Citation Index. Based on the collected data the following discussions are made.

ANALYSIS AND INTERPRETATION

The distributions of the research output by the authors from Madurai Kamaraj University that are available in Indian Citation Index were analyzed in table 1.

Year Wise Distribution of Published Articles Vs Citations

Table 1. Year Wise Distribution of Published Articles Vs Citations

S. No.	*Year*	*Articles*	*%*	*Citation*	*%*	*Citation Density*	*Article/ Citation*
1	2004	23	5.56	13	6.60	0.565	2
2	2005	38	9.18	50	25.38	1.316	1
3	2006	35	8.45	24	12.18	0.686	1
4	2007	34	8.21	18	9.14	0.529	2
5	2008	45	10.87	17	8.63	0.378	3
6	2009	31	7.49	24	12.18	0.774	1

7	2010	27	6.52	7	3.55	0.259	4
8	2011	45	10.87	17	8.63	0.378	3
9	2012	40	9.66	14	7.11	0.350	3
10	2013	29	7.01	2	1.02	0.069	15
11	2014	35	8.45	7	3.55	0.200	5
12	2015	32	7.73	4	2.03	0.125	8
	Total	414	100	197	100	5.629	48

The above Table shows that the year wise distribution of articles published by the various authors from Madurai Kamaraj University. From 2004 to 2015, 414 articles were published which are indexed in Indian Citation Index. Among the 414, maximum of 45(10.87%) articles published in 2008 & 2011 and minimum of 23(5.56%) articles published in 2004. Based on the citation during the period 197 citations were made. Among the 197 Citations, maximum of 50(25.38%) citations in 2005 and minimum number of citations 4(2.03%) in 2015, was identified.

Year Wise Distribution of Cited Articles & Cited Density

Table 2. Year Wise Distribution of Cited Articles & Cited Density

S. No.	*Year*	*Cited Articles*	*%*	*Cited Density*	*Article/Cited*
1	2004	10	9.35	0.435	2.300
2	2005	22	20.56	0.579	1.727
3	2006	11	10.28	0.314	3.182
4	2007	10	9.35	0.294	3.400
5	2008	11	10.28	0.244	4.091
6	2009	9	8.41	0.290	3.444
7	2010	4	3.74	0.148	6.750
8	2011	11	10.28	0.244	4.091
9	2012	7	6.54	0.175	5.714
10	2013	2	1.87	0.069	14.500
11	2014	7	6.54	0.200	5.000
12	2015	3	2.80	0.094	10.667
	Total	107	100	3.086	64.866

The above Table presents the year wise distribution of Cited articles, Cited density and Article/ Cited articles published by the various authors from Madurai Kamaraj University. From 2004 to 2015, 107 cited articles were available which are indexed in Indian Citation Index. Among the cited articles maximum of 22(20.56%) in 2005 and minimum of 2 (1.87%) cited articles in 2013. Based on the cited density during the period maximum of 0.579 in 2005 and minimum number of 0.069 in 2013, was identified.

Author Wise Distribution of Articles And Citations (Top 15)

Table 3. Author-wise Distribution of Articles and Citations (Top 15)

Sl. No.	*Author*	*Articles*	*Citation*	*Citation Density*
1	Srinivasan C	24	7	0.292
2	Gunasekaran P	13	12	0.857
3	Muthusubramanian Shanmugam	12	4	0.333
4	Saraswathi R	12	1	0.083
5	Paliwal Kailash	11	9	0.818
6	Ramu A	11	10	0.909
7	Ramesh P	9	2	0.222
8	Karuppanapandian T	9	6	0.667
9	Chandrasekaran S	8	18	2.250
10	Swamy P S	8	16	2.000
11	Saravanan Sivaperuman	7	2	0.286
12	Ramachandran K	7	8	1.143
13	Renuga G	7	4	0.571
14	Muthusubramanian P	7	2	0.286
15	Murugesan A	7	5	0.714
	Total	152	106	11.431

The above table reveals that the author wise distribution of the articles published and citations are available in the Indian Citation Index. Only we consider in the top fifteen authors. Among the 15, Srinivasan .C occupied the first position with 24 articles and 7 citations followed by author Gunasekaran P in the second position with 13 articles and 12citations and Muthusubramanian Shanmugam in the third position with 12 articles and 4 citations (Ranked by Articles only). In the case of highest citations Chandrasekaran S is in the first position with 18 citations and Swamy P S occupies the second position with 16 citations and Gunasekaran P occupies the third position with 12 citations.

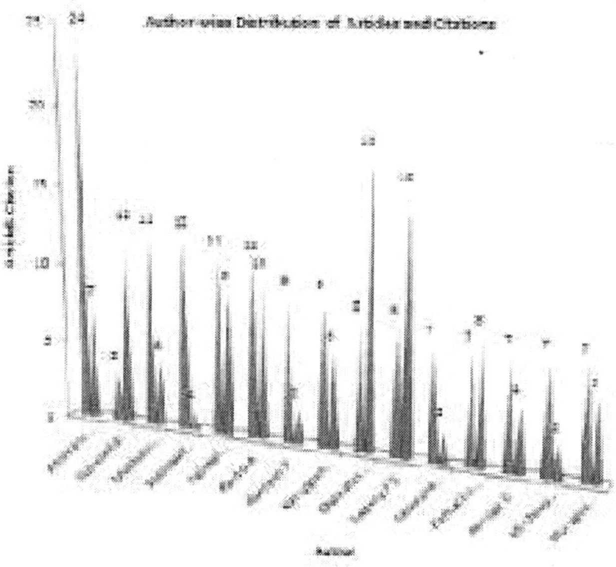

Subject Wise Distribution of Cited Articles (Top 15)

Table 4. Subject Wise Distribution of Cited Articles (TOP 15)

S. No.	*Subject Category*	*Articles*	*Citation*
1	Biological Science	96	61
2	Chemistry	78	16
3	General Science & Technology	74	51
4	Environmental Science	55	24
5	Botany	26	12

6	Biotechnology	21	13
7	Pharmacology & Pharmaceutical Science	21	7
8	Engineering Science &Technology	20	2
9	Library & Information Science	19	6
10	Physics	18	5
11	Business & Marketing	16	4
12	Health Science	16	2
13	Management	15	0
14	Pollution	14	5
15	Social Science	14	4
	Total	503	212

The above Table presents the top 15 subjects it includes various articles published and cited from the Madurai Kamaraj University that are available in the Indian Citation Index. As per the sources available in the Indian Citation Index, the articles 96 from Biological Science is in the first rank, 78 articles from Chemistry with second rank and 74 articles from General Science & Technology subject in third rank were identified. It is revealed from the table that Biological Science subject has the highest citations 61 when comparing to other subjects.

Distribution of Top 15 Cited Journals

Table 5. Distribution of Top 15 Cited Journals

Sl. No.	*Publications*	*Articles*	*Citation*
1	Current Science	58	44
2	Indian Journal of Chemistry Section B - Organic Including Medicinal	22	5
3	Journal of Plant Biology	14	8
4	Bulletin of Materials Science	12	12
5	Pollution Research	12	5
6	Indian Journal of Marketing	11	4
7	Asian Journal of Microbiology Biotechnology & Environmental Sciences	10	5

8	Journal of Chemical Science	10	0
9	Asian Journal of Chemistry	8	2
10	Indian Journal of Biotechnology	8	7
11	Indian Journal of Experimental Biology	8	12
12	Indian Journal of Heterocyclic Chemistry	8	2
13	Indian Journal of Science And Technology	8	3
14	International Journal of Chem. tech Research	8	1
15	Indian Journal of Environmental Protection	7	9
	Total	**204**	**119**

The data presented in the above table shows the top 15 journals articles published and cited by authors in Madurai Kamaraj University. Among the top 15, Current Science occupies the first place with 58articles the second place in Indian Journal of Chemistry Section B - Organic Including Medicinal with 22 articles and the third place in Journal of Plant Biology with14 based on the article publications. Based on the Current Science occupies the first position with 44 citations and Bulletin of Materials Science and Indian Journal of Experimental Biology is in the second position with 12 citations.

Distribution of Document Type

Table 6. Distribution of Document Type

S. No.	*Document Type*	*Articles*	*%*	*Citation*	*%*
1	Research Article	349	84.30	141	71.57
2	Short Communication	28	6.76	29	14.72
3	Editorial	14	3.38	6	3.05
4	Review Article	11	2.66	17	8.63
5	Case Study	6	1.45	3	1.52
6	Research Note	6	1.45	1	0.51
	Total	414	100	197	100

The above table expresses the distribution of document type based on the articles published from Madurai Kamaraj University. It shows among the 414 articles, which includes 349 (84.30%) Research Articles, 28(6.76%) Short Communication and 14 (3.38%) editorial type. Among the 197 Citations, which include 141 (71.57%) Research Articles type followed by 29 (14.72%) Short Communication type and 17 (8.63%) from Review articles. It is concluded that the highest articles and citations are from research article type of documents.

CONCLUSION

Indian Citation Index to offer an easy-to-use, reliable bibliographic and citation database to users. During the study period among the published articles 414, maximum of 45(10.87%) articles published in 2008&2011 and minimum of 23(5.56%) articles published in 2004.Based on the citation during the period 197 citations were made. The maximum of 50(25.38%) citations in 2005 and minimum number of citations 4(2.03%) in 2015, was identified. The cited articles study reveals that the maximum of 22(20.56%) in 2005 and minimum of 2(1.87%) cited articles in 2013.Based on the cited density shows that the maximum of 0.579 in 2005 and minimum number of 0.069 in 2013, was identified. The Author Wise Distribution of Articles and Citations study tells that the author Srinivasan C occupied the first position with 24 articles and 7 citations followed by author Gunasekaran P in the second position with 13 articles and 12 citations and Muthusubramanian Shanmugam in the third position with 12 articles and 4 citations (Ranked by Articles only). In the case of highest citations Chandrasekaran S is in the first position with 18 citations and Swamy P S occupies the second position with 16 citations and Gunasekaran P occupies the third position with 12 citations. The Subject wise distribution of cited articles study reveals that 96 articles from Biological Science is in the first rank followed by Chemistry with 78 is in second rank and 74 articles from General Science &

Technology subject in third rank were identified. It proves from the table that Biological Science subject has the highest citations of 61 when comparing to other subjects. The Distribution of Top 15 Cited Journals depicts that, the Current Science occupies the first place with 58 articles followed by the Indian Journal of Chemistry Section B - Organic Including Medicinal is in second place with 22 articles and the third place in Journal of Plant Biology with14 based on the article publications. Based on the citations Current Science occupies the first position with 44 citations and Bulletin of Materials Science and Indian Journal of Experimental Biology is in the second position with 12 citations. The distribution of document type study proves that the Research Articles are 349(84.30%) followed by Short Communication with 28(6.76%) and 14(3.38%) editorial type. Among the 197 Citations, which include 141(71.57%) Research Articles type followed by 29(14.72%) Short Communication type and 17(8.63%) from Review articles. It is concluded that the highest articles and citations are from research article type of documents.

REFERENCES

1. Nicholas David and Ritchie Maureen(1978). Literature and Bibliometrics. London: Clive Bingley.
2. Potter W.G., (1981) Introduction to bibliometrics, Library Trends, 30, 5, http://www.myjurnal.my/filebank/published_article / 17760/4.pdf .
3. Mooghali A. et al. (2011) Scientometric Analysis of the Scientometric Literature, International Journal of Information Science and Management, 9(1), 19-31.
4. Karpagam R. et al. (2011) .Mapping of Nano science and nanotechnology research in India: a scientometric analysis, 1990-2009, Scientometrics, 89(2), 501-522
5. Abramo Giovanni, (2011).National research assessment exercises: a comparison of peer review and bibliometrics rankings. Scientometrics, 89(3), 929-941
6. Lapon-Kandelshein, Esther and Prebor, Gilla, (2011). Bibliographical research in the study of Hebrew printing: a bibliometric analysis, Scientometrics, 88(3), 899-913

7. Krampen G., Eye A. and Schui G., (2011).Forecasting trends of development of psychology from a bibliometric perspective, Scientometrics, 87(3), 687-694

8. Kumar suchetan, Tiwari Charu and Deepu Mahija, (2012), contribution to Indian sociology: A Bibliometric study, Language in India,

9. S. Dhanavandan and M. Tamizhchelvan , (2014), Citations and Self citations of Indian Authors in Library and Information Science: A Study Based Indian Citation Index (ICI). *International Journal of Academic Library and Information Science*, 2(9), 138-144.